CREATING A VOLUNTEER-FRIENDLY CHURCH CULTURE

Marlene Wilson, Author and General Editor

Group's Volunteer Leadership Series™
Volume 1
Group's Church Volunteer Central™

D1367812

Loveland, Colorado

BR
115
.V65
W55
v. 1

Group's Volunteer Leadership Series™, Volume 1

Creating a Volunteer-Friendly Church Culture

Copyright © 2004 Group Publishing, Inc.

Visit our Web site: **www.grouppublishing.com**

Credits
Author: Marlene Wilson
Editor: Mikal Keefer
General Editor: Marlene Wilson
Chief Creative Officer: Joani Schultz
Art Director: Nathan Hindman
Cover Designer: Jeff Storm
Production Manager: Peggy Naylor

Unless otherwise noted, Scripture taken from the HOLY BIBLE, NEW INTERNATIONAL VERSION®. Copyright © 1973, 1978, 1984 International Bible Society. Used by permission of Zondervan Publishing House. All rights reserved.

Produced with the assistance of The Livingstone Corporation (www.LivingstoneCorp.com). Project staff includes Chris Hudson, Ashley Taylor, Mary Horner Collins, Joel Bartlett, Cheryl Dunlop, Mary Larsen, and Rosalie Krusemark.

Library of Congress Cataloging-in-Publication Data

Wilson, Marlene.
Creating a volunteer-friendly church culture / Marlene Wilson.—1st American
        hardbound ed.
        p. cm. — (Group's volunteer leadership series ; v. 1)
        ISBN 0-7644-2745-8 (alk. paper)
        1. Voluntarism—Religious aspects—Christianity. 2. Christian leadership. I. Group
Publishing. II. Title. III. Series.
BR115.V64W55 2003
253'.7—dc22   2003022118

10 9 8 7 6 5 4 3 2 1   12 11 10 09 08 07 06 05 04

Printed in the United States of America.

Contents

Introduction

Does this picture remind you of your church?

Imagine walking into your church on a Sunday morning and seeing a beehive of activity . . .

- Classes hum along with smiling teachers ready to greet students.
- The music team is tuned up and ready to go.
- The coffee pots are filled and percolating.
- Visitors filter in through the doors because someone stopped by to visit newcomers in the community with fresh bread and invitations.

And it's all happening because at your church volunteers are in place and serving others. There's no scrambling around at the last minute—everything is right on schedule, right on time, right on target, and completely relaxed.

> "Imagine . . . everyone is a volunteer."

Imagine attending a church board meeting that's sharply focused, well-organized, and attended by people who can't think of anything else they'd rather be doing. People who are energized by the mission of the church and the purpose of the board.

And everyone around the table on that Thursday night is a volunteer.

Imagine walking down the hallway at church, glancing into offices where individuals and teams are busily pulling together a slideshow for next week's worship service . . . providing counseling for a man who's in emotional pain . . . planning a youth group retreat . . . and rehearsing a drama that will introduce a sermon later in the week.

And everyone—in each room—is a volunteer.

Does it seem like a dream to have so many volunteers so involved in important ministry? In some churches it is just a dream . . . but it doesn't need to stay a dream.

This Volunteer Leadership Series will help you turn your dreams of volunteer involvement into reality. There's nothing magical about the process you'll discover in this series. Many of the principles and procedures are straight out of the business world where they've worked for decades.

Some are from the nonprofit sector where they've worked equally well for just as long.

And some are from churches like yours that are a bit further along in the journey of creating a culture where volunteering is more than an obligation—it's a joy.

Throughout these books you'll discover a process that has taken me—and many, many colleagues—35 years to refine. It's tested and it works, and you'll see the results if you implement all of it in your church.

Maybe you're the pastor and you have a vision for a time when you're not the only one who's doing the work of ministry. You want to see volunteers join in the work of the church so you can have at least a little time with your family.

"See volunteers join in the work of the church."

Maybe you're the Christian Education Director or Youth Director and you'd like to see enough volunteers signed up to cover the small group or outreach ministry you'd love to start. You have a vision for what your area of ministry could be, and you're tired of settling for less.

Or maybe you're a board member or other volunteer who knows the fulfillment of being involved and used by God in ministry. You want to invite others who are now filling pews to be filling volunteer roles instead.

No matter what your role in your church, imagine with me for a moment . . .

Imagine the power that would be unleashed if everyone offered to serve in an appropriate volunteer role. How much could your church accomplish? What might you do that you simply can't do now?

Imagine how the members of your church would grow if they were actively, intentionally serving God and growing in their faith. If everyone came together on Sunday not for a quick spiritual pick-me-up, but instead with exciting stories to share about how God is using them.

Imagine how your church would grow if you had the reputation of being the place where people don't just talk about their faith, but work together to make things happen in your community. What if church members were constantly forming groups to enthusiastically meet real needs of real people? How packed would your new members' class be? And how deep would you be growing in your faith?

If you have a vision for your church that includes any of the scenarios I've sketched above, you need a fully functioning, healthy volunteer ministry. It won't be enough to keep improving your church's programs, or to count on a remarkable pastor to draw new people to your worship services.

Excellent programs and a charismatic leader may help your church grow in attendance, but they won't help your church members grow deep in their faith or be satisfied with their spiritual growth. That takes involvement in ministry—which requires a volunteer program that's working.

Don't believe me? I'll prove it, then.

> "You need a fully functioning, healthy volunteer ministry."

In a *Leadership* journal article, Eric Swanson reported about a survey he gave his church to determine if there was a relationship between ministering to others and spiritual growth. Swanson asked the question, "To what extent has your ministry or service to others affected your spiritual growth?" and received a 92 percent "positive" response. When Swanson dug deeper and asked how service to others compared with other spiritual disciplines such as Bible study and prayer, 63 percent of respondents reported service to others was equally significant in their spiritual growth, and 24 percent of respondents said service to others was more significant than Bible study or prayer![1]

But how do you involve the membership of your church in significant service and ministry when many people don't express the slightest interest in getting involved? There are ways to encourage that change, and in this series we'll walk you through that process.

> **"It's your vision . . . that sets the direction of your entire volunteer ministry."**

It starts with building a firm foundation on solid biblical thinking about volunteers and volunteerism. There are several theologies you must embrace concerning how God has designed people and the church if you expect to see volunteerism grow in your congregation.

Later in this volume you'll do a quick assessment of how "volunteer-friendly" your church culture is and identify obstacles that might be blocking your progress.

Finally, you'll craft a vision for where you want to be.

This first volume is all about understanding what you believe as a church, where you're starting your journey, and where you want to go. It may feel as if you're not diving quickly enough into shaping up your volunteer program, and you may be tempted to skip over this "vision stuff."

Don't do it.

It's your vision for where you want to go that sets the direction of your entire volunteer ministry. This is the foundation on which you'll build your program. Skipping these key steps is like staking out a place to build a house on a beach and building your house on sand—and we all know how that turns out.

Are you ready to launch or expand your volunteer program? Ready for changes that will dramatically increase the number of people in your church who are enthusiastically serving?

Wonderful! Let's begin . . . with you and what you believe about volunteers.

1. Eric Swanson, "What You Get from Giving" sidebar in " 'Great to Good' Churches," *Leadership*, Spring 2003, Vol. XXIV, No. 2, 38.

ONE
The Biblical Foundation for Volunteerism

What do you believe about volunteerism and volunteers? Here's a quick look at three theologies that are the foundation of volunteer leadership in the church.

I love the question *what if?*

When I ask *what if?* I can begin picturing what tomorrow might be like. Asking that question invites me to cooperate with God in imagining a vision for the future.

Your church will have a future—next week, next year, and beyond. Wouldn't it be best if your church had the future you prefer? One that's grounded in God's will for your congregation, that's spiritually healthy, and that's moving forward to do God's will in your community?

When it comes to involving volunteers in your church, there's no secret about what God wants to accomplish. It's all there in the Bible, and it is reflected in three interrelated theologies. Let's explore these together. As we go, think about your church and how you're living out these theologies.

The Priesthood of All Believers

True or False?—God intends for every member of your church to be active in ministry.

True! According to Scripture, we're all called to be active in the ministry of the church. God never intended for church to be a spectator sport. Just the opposite is what God has in mind, as we see in this passage:

> *But you are a chosen people, a royal priesthood, a holy nation, a people belonging to God, that you may declare the praises of him who called you out of darkness into his wonderful light. (1 Peter 2:9)*

That "royal priesthood" is for all Christians, not just professional clergy. Men and women—we're all part of the priesthood of all believers.

Age doesn't have anything to do with it, either. In the same way we're not expected to retire from service when we get to the age of 65, neither are we too young to be involved when we're in sixth grade. When you think of who's been called by God to be involved in ministry, include your entire membership.

When someone walks into your church, is it evident that you believe everyone has a place in ministry? Or is significant ministry done just by the paid staff or a handful of people? Maybe ministry is being done by just a few people because no one else will do it, but what's your preference? Does your church have an openness to lay people assuming ministry roles?

"Is it evident that you believe everyone has a place in ministry?"

Because if that's God's expectation—that lay people will have ministry opportunity—we'd better be providing those opportunities. Failing to do so only cripples the church.

I think there's ample evidence in Scripture that God is looking for us all to roll up our sleeves and get involved. When we made a commitment to God, he made a claim on our lives.

Paul wrote:

> *Do you not know that your body is a temple of the Holy Spirit, who is in you, whom you have received from God? You are not your own; you were bought at a price. (1 Corinthians 6:19-20a)*

In the book of Romans we read:

> *What then? Shall we sin because we are not under law but under grace? By no means! Don't you know that when you*

offer yourselves to someone to obey him as slaves, you are slaves to the one whom you obey—whether you are slaves to sin, which leads to death, or to obedience, which leads to righteousness? But thanks be to God that, though you used to be slaves to sin, you wholeheartedly obeyed the form of teaching to which you were entrusted. (Romans 6:15-17)

Bought at a price.

Slaves.

Those words communicate that God owns us. He's paid for us. We're his. If he's got work to do, it's clear that we're all on his payroll. He wants to use us all.

Not everyone will preach, teach, or sing in the choir. But all Christians are supposed to be doing something that fits within their unique blend of abilities, skills, and passions. It's really not optional. Priesthood is all about *doing* something as well as *believing* something.

> "Priesthood is all about *doing* something as well as *believing* something."

What's the evidence in your church that you embrace the priesthood of all believers? Do church members see volunteers serving in significant and varied roles? Do they see every category of person involved in ministry of some sort?

If not, is your church willing to change?

By the way, here's the first place you should make changes: in the expectations of your leaders and lay membership.

When Jesus recruited his disciples, he called them to leave their businesses and families. It cost those fishermen something to follow Jesus. It often costs us little to follow Jesus, at least in the Western world. People expect to go to church and drop money in the offering plate, but that's about it.

So no wonder lay people look surprised when we explain they also need to serve in a ministry. It may be the first time they've heard they're required to do anything beyond showing up and writing a check.

We tell people all about the Savior Jesus. We teach about how Jesus saves people from their sins, loves them, and is preparing a place for them in heaven.

But we sometimes forget to mention much about the Lord Jesus.

The Lord Jesus calls everyone who follows him into the royal priesthood, where service and discipleship are more than theories—they're expectations. Joining a church isn't an invitation to retire; it's enlistment in an organization that's actively serving God. If you're going to expect people to volunteer in service, say so up front in your teaching and preaching.

- *Does* your church invite every member to be in appropriate ministry somehow?

- *Is* there a place for each person in your church to do ministry? Are you open to an influx of volunteers?

The Giftedness of Each Child of God

The Bible tells us that every believer can do ministry in some way. Each person has important work to do in the church regardless of gender, age, or education.

Here's what Paul wrote:

> For we are God's workmanship, created in Christ Jesus to do good works, which God prepared in advance for us to do. (Ephesians 2:10)

And again he wrote:

> And in the church God has appointed first of all apostles, second prophets, third teachers, then workers of miracles, also those having gifts of healing, those able to help others, those with gifts of administration, and those speaking in different kinds of tongues. Are all apostles? Are all prophets? Are all teachers? Do all work miracles? Do all have gifts of healing? Do all speak in tongues? Do all interpret? But eagerly desire the greater gifts. And now I will show you the most excellent way. (1 Corinthians 12:28-31)

Finally, consider this passage in Romans:

> If it is serving, let him serve; if it is teaching, let him teach; if it is encouraging, let him encourage; if it is contributing to the needs of others, let him give generously; if it is leadership, let him govern diligently; if it is showing mercy, let him do it cheerfully. (Romans 12:7-8)

Clearly, believers' God-given abilities, skills, and passions are to be used to build up the body of Christ and to glorify God. Those are the truths wrapped up in the theology of "the giftedness of each child of God."

> "*Our* job is to help people discover where to put those abilities, skills, and passions to use."

Our job is to help people discover where to put those abilities, skills, and passions to use. We need to do it for the health of the church and also for the spiritual health of individual believers.

But before you embark on that journey, you need to decide:

- *Do* you believe each person in your church has something valuable to contribute?

- *Are* you willing to help people who aren't sure what they can offer to discover ways to serve?

- *Will* your church make room for people to serve in ways that align with their abilities, skills, and passions?

The Whole Body of Christ

In the same way each believer has a God-given ability, skill, or passion to use in ministry, each believer has a particular function in the body of Christ. We all fit *somewhere*, but we don't all fit *everywhere*. There's a big difference.

The theology of "the whole body of Christ" acknowledges that each member of your church has something to offer, but it's a specific something. People aren't interchangeable; you can't just move them around on the organizational chart. Someone God has designed to be an empathic, caring people-helper isn't going to thrive in a volunteer role that's designed to enter data on a spreadsheet. If someone's a hand, he or she won't fit a role designed for a foot.

The programs in our churches are enhanced, changed, and expanded when we discover our church members' gifts and abilities. We get the right people in the right jobs, and everyone benefits.

Consider these passages . . .

> It was he who gave some to be apostles, some to be prophets, some to be evangelists, and some to be pastors and teachers, to prepare God's people for works of service, so that the body of Christ may be built up until we all reach unity in the faith and in the knowledge of the Son of God and become mature, attaining to the whole measure of the fullness of Christ. (Ephesians 4:11-13)

> Now the body is not made up of one part but of many. If the foot should say, "Because I am not a hand, I do not belong to the body," it would not for that reason cease to be part of the body. And if the ear should say, "Because I am not an eye, I do not belong to the body," it would not for that reason cease to be part of the body. If the whole body were an eye, where would the sense of hearing be? If the whole body were an ear, where would the sense of smell be? But in fact God has arranged the parts in the body, every one of them, just as he wanted them to be. If they were all one part, where would the body be? As it is, there are many parts, but one body.
> The eye cannot say to the hand, "I don't need you!" And the head cannot say to the feet, "I don't need you!" On the contrary, those parts of the body that seem to be weaker are indispensable, and the parts that we think are less honorable we treat with special honor. And the parts that are unpresentable are treated with special modesty, while our presentable parts need no special treatment. But God has combined the members of the body and has given greater honor to the parts that lacked it, so that there should be no division in the body, but that its parts should have equal concern for each other. If one part suffers, every part suffers with it; if one part is honored, every part rejoices with it. Now you are the body of Christ, and each one of you is a part of it." (1 Corinthians 12:14-27)

- *Are* you willing to encourage people to minister within the constraints of their unique abilities, talents, and passions? If not, how do you expect those volunteers to be successful and fulfilled?

- *Are* you willing to not do programs if you can't staff them appropriately?

Now let me ask a few *what-if* questions about your church—and mine.

What if we took seriously the implications of our theology when it comes to volunteerism in our churches?

What if we reflected biblical principles in our policies and procedures when it comes to recruiting and using volunteers in our own churches?

What if we learned from our brothers and sisters in Christ who have found ways to make volunteerism joyful—and we put their experience to good use in our churches?

I'll tell you what will happen in most churches when *what if* becomes reality: We'll see dramatic and profound changes.

That's because in most churches, volunteerism is suffering. Most of the work of the church is done by the hired staff or a small group of volunteers. The vast majority of church members sit and watch, or, at best, are peripherally involved. They certainly don't find any meaning in their service through the church.

Wouldn't it be wonderful if serving in and through the church became the norm instead of the exception? What if the days when you had to beg for volunteers faded into a distant memory because people were actively seeking to serve? Wouldn't that be a welcome change?

> "Not one volunteer program changed overnight."

The question is: How do we get from where we are to where we want to go?

This series will help you, but it's a journey and a process. There's no pixie dust you can sprinkle on your church directory and find that, suddenly, calls will pour in from willing volunteers. I've worked with many, many churches to improve their volunteer programs, and not one of them changed overnight.

But the churches that grew successful volunteer programs all had three things in common, and this is the place to briefly talk about them.

1. They approached the process prayerfully.

Sometimes the apathy in the pews toward doing the work of the church is a spiritual issue. It can't be fixed by doing a better job writing volunteer job descriptions. Nor can it be fixed by initiating a new process. It has to be fixed through what I call a "heart transplant," a renewing and refreshing of the heart.

Your church might just need a change of heart about serving God and serving the church. And that gets fixed through prayer and through sharing God's vision for what your church could be as God's representative in your community.

Will you commit to pray for your church? For your leaders, for your vision and mission, and for the members of your church who are willing volunteers—and those who aren't? They all need prayer.

In volume 2 we'll dig a little deeper into this facet of volunteer program development.

2. They embraced the entire process.

I can't stress this enough: *You must embrace the entire process we'll be describing.* If you pick and choose an idea here and a process there, you'll see improvement. It's all good stuff and it works. But you'll be sticking an adhesive bandage over a broken bone.

I expect you're already doing many things right. Were I to visit your church I'd find lots of things to praise. If you're like most people who are responsible for finding, recruiting, training, and maintaining volunteers, you have strong communication skills. You're already experiencing some success at the process I just described.

The problem is that the process I just mentioned—finding, recruiting, training, and maintaining volunteers—is missing several key components. You may be excellent at all those things; you've still skipped important steps. Until you have them all, your effectiveness and results will be compromised. Your success will be limited, and you'll have to work harder.

In this series, we'll give you those missing pieces. But please trust me when I say they're all important. You can't skip past any of them. There are no shortcuts in the process. We've already weeded out the fluff and extra steps.

What's left is a process for bringing volunteers on board that assures you—and the volunteers—that you'll have the right people in the right positions.

3. They built programs on a solid biblical foundation.

The three theologies we examined aren't new. We've all nodded in agreement as we've heard them preached and taught. But do we *believe* them? And if we *do* believe them, are the actions and attitudes expressed in our churches consistent with them?

Those three theologies are fundamental to your church's volunteer program. They reflect God's values when it comes to our doing kingdom work and how he has designed the church. When we let the values in these theologies slip, some terrible things can happen. Things that actually discourage volunteerism.

Consider this example of how a church leader chose to value a program over the people who were in his congregation . . .

The Little Drama Team That Couldn't

The pastor of a small church attended a conference hosted by a California megachurch. The pastor noticed how well drama was used in the megachurch's worship service, so he did a little investigating.

It turned out the drama ministry was comprised of a team of more than 50 people. They rehearsed regularly and performed two plays each year. They also sang musical numbers and performed skits each week that reinforced the sermon theme. They even had a sub-team of writers who did nothing but create original skits for the actors to perform.

The pastor couldn't wait to pull together a similar team back home. He just knew it would revolutionize his church's worship experiences.

So, two weeks after the pastor returned, he called a meeting for everyone interested in drama ministry. Two people showed up . . . and one was a junior high student who'd never been in a play.

The pastor made it a personal priority to get a team organized.

He made another announcement and did a bit of personal recruiting. That got his team up to five. Still not enough.

So the pastor called a few of the perpetual volunteers— people who always said yes when asked directly—and twisted their arms. Reluctantly, two of those people joined, too, giving the team a total of seven members. Not ideal, but for a church of one hundred, not bad. Not bad at all.

> "Most of the drama team was made up of the wrong people for the volunteer role."

It wasn't bad—it was worse than bad. The first skit was a disaster. Some of the team forgot lines. Others got stage fright and simply stood in place. The few people with an aptitude for drama couldn't pull the skit out of a tailspin. The effect was powerful—but not in the way the pastor wanted.

What went wrong? Plenty, but at heart it came down to this: *Most of the drama team was made up of the wrong people for the volunteer role.*

The pastor did respect the priesthood of all believers theology—everyone was invited to participate in this ministry. But the pastor didn't respect the unique giftings of church members or their function in the body of Christ.

TWO
Navigating the Rapids of Change

Launching or improving the volunteer leadership process in your church forces change. Here's how to deal with it.

I know that initiating change in a church can be a difficult process. It may feel that now isn't the time to go through the pain of changing the way you interact with volunteers; you'll just make a few adjustments to your current volunteer process and hope that works.

As gently as I can, let me suggest that won't work. If you want to experience real change, you're going to have to do more than fiddle with a few loose wires. You've got to dig in and rebuild the engine. You've got to commit to making true changes, and it's going to take time.

My question for you: If not now, when will you make the changes? After you again experience a volunteer drought? After another batch of volunteers grows discouraged and quits? After yet another staff member moans about how nobody seems to care at your church?

Now is the time to start making changes. Today.

I frequently present workshops and speeches on the theme of the changing world of volunteerism. Often I title these speeches "Suddenly It's Tomorrow." This is based on a lesson I learned from a five-year-old—the very best teacher when it comes to dealing with the timing of change.

I was at a board of directors meeting and we were on a coffee break, relaxing and chatting. A board member shared an experience his wife had just had as a kindergarten teacher. On the first day of school she asked, "Can anyone tell me what day it is?"

A bright-eyed little tyke raised her hand and declared, "It's tomorrow."

The kindergartner may not have had a firm grasp on the logistics of time, but she certainly understood the truth of time: It *is* tomorrow. Time is rushing by, and if we want things to be different in the future we've got to act now to create the tomorrow we're envisioning.

> **"It *is* tomorrow. . . We've got to act now to create the tomorrow we're envisioning."**

I expect you're feeling some urgency about changing how your church deals with volunteers. That's why you're reading this book. Honor that urgency—in most churches it's past time to initiate change. There's nothing to be gained by waiting longer to get started. Things won't get better by themselves, you know. Not without someone like you diving in and initiating change.

Tell me: If you had a friend who was experiencing a major health issue, would you suggest that she wait until things grew even worse before seeing a doctor? Of course not.

Would you suggest she live with the pain indefinitely because it might get better eventually? No—you'd urge her to get the help she needed right away.

Listen: If your church is experiencing pain in working with volunteers, it won't get better without intervention. You must act to initiate change, or you'll be stuck where you are today—forever. Is that what you want?

Let me suggest two more *what-ifs* for your consideration:

What if we took God seriously enough to act on the theology we declare—even though it means dramatically changing how we do ministry?

What if we honored the urgency we feel to see change happen and we actually started initiating that change?

It boggles my mind what the church could become!

Let me share with you the story of a church that has managed to implement the process we'll be sharing with you: the Community Church of Joy in Glendale, Arizona. You may know them as a megachurch that has more than 10,000 members. That's who they are today, but when the church's pastor, Walt Kallestad, went to the church in 1978 there were just 200 members.

When Walt arrived, he and the church leadership discerned that they were uniquely called to missions, to reaching out to the unchurched. That's a mission and vision that energized some members, but alienated others who wanted to maintain the status quo.

Once the vision was articulated, Walt saw some of the membership leave. It was a cost the church was willing to pay to get the entire church membership onto the same page and moving the same direction.

To grow 50-fold in 25 years requires a church to stay open to change. What works when a church is at a membership of 400 won't necessarily work when membership reaches 4,000.

> "Pastor Kallestad learned to change his language so he could connect with unchurched people."

One change that came up on Pastor Kallestad's radar screen was a need for language to be friendly to unchurched people. Much of the traditional church jargon was a mystery to someone not raised in the church.

The woman who is in charge of the women's ministry was once one of those unchurched visitors. She kept coming back, even though at times she was uncertain what certain words meant. So she started keeping a list, and when the opportunity arose she asked Pastor Kallestad to define the terms. Words like "evangelism" and "atonement" held no meaning for her, but she suspected they must be important—they were always coming up in sermons.

After having to explain the meaning of church words a few times, Pastor Kallestad learned to change his language so he could connect with unchurched people. Because that was the stated mission of Community Church of Joy, learning a new way to communicate was worth the effort.

Christian education courses were adapted so new members and visitors who had no Bible background at all could participate. When someone doesn't know if the book of Luke is in the Old Testament or New Testament, that changes how you approach teaching.

> "The work of ministry had to be passed to lay people, . . . or there would be chaos."

In time, it became apparent another change had to happen, too, and it concerned volunteers.

People with no church background—and there was an ever-increasing number of them involved in the congregation—were difficult to recruit as volunteers. They had no history of volunteering in the church. They had not grown up seeing their parents participate as volunteers. To these new members, attending a worship experience was like attending a play put on by a community theater: They were the audience. It never occurred to newly churched people that there was a role they could play in making things happen.

I received a call from Pastor Kallestad just before the church moved to a new campus. The congregation was already nearing 10,000 members, and church leadership expected they'd experience a new growth surge after the relocation.

Pastor Kallestad said, "We can't do it with our present structure." The work of ministry had to be passed to lay people more effectively than was happening, or there would be chaos.

Keep in mind the church was growing. Good things were happening. Lots of churches hungry to experience the same sort of growth were visiting, taking notes. And the church already had lots of volunteers involved. The church leadership could have sat back and rested on its laurels.

But instead they felt an urgency to move ahead. To be even more effective. To be sure that the three theologies they supported with words were also supported in action.

I'd like to share a letter I received from the Community Church of Joy staff after they put in place the process we'll discuss with you in this book series. I think what they've experienced will be an encouragement for you to see the process through.

> We knew we needed to move to a new level of excellence in our volunteer ministry, but we weren't sure how to make that move. We knew the change would need to be monumental. . . . We enlisted Marlene to do three things:
>
> 1. Help us find a person to serve as our "Director of Volunteer Ministries."
>
> 2. Help us design a strategic plan for volunteer ministry at Joy.
>
> 3. Train our key leaders so that we could carry on the ministry.
>
> All three of those goals have been accomplished. With Marlene's help, our Director of Volunteer Ministries, Joyce Pokorny, and a core team have developed the following teams:
>
> **The Connections Team**—volunteers who meet with new members to assist individuals to serve and grow at Joy.
>
> **The Recognition/Retention Team**—which implements an ongoing program for the recognition of volunteers, including an annual recognition event (a dinner with a guest speaker) and the commissioning of volunteers during a worship service.
>
> **The Ministry Liaison Team**—which is comprised of volunteers who represent individual ministries, and who welcome new volunteers, train them, and follow up to make sure placement was a good fit.
>
> **The Training Team**—which trains our staff in areas of recognition, empowerment, and recruitment/retention.
>
> **The Data Management Team**—which provides support for all information received from volunteers regarding their gifts, talents, abilities, and passions.

The **Special Events Teams**—which implements special events such as the Celebration of Lights event and the Celebration of Easter event. Volunteers who join the special events teams will then be followed up for next steps of service. (This has been an awesome way to connect individuals to ministry!)

Through the coaching and mentoring of our Director of Volunteer Ministries, our Missions Ministry has increased volunteer involvement from 100 volunteers to more than 500 volunteers. Teams have been put in place for Feeding the Homeless, Habitat for Humanity, Acts of Kindness, and much more.

Our director shares, "There is no way I could have done this myself. I have learned to empower and release our volunteers for service."

Volunteers' lives have been changed, too. Once individuals have stepped up to volunteer and have served, they want to grow and know Jesus Christ through Bible studies, worship, and "going deeper."

As our key leaders have been trained, our church culture has begun to shift toward becoming better at equipping and releasing lay people into significant ministry.

Before Marlene helped us make the changes I've noted, we had about 80 people in volunteer ministry. Today more than 1,700 people serve at Joy, and through Joy in our community. We're so grateful to God for this breakthrough. Equipping our people has changed us, and is changing our community!

Gratefully,

Pastor Paul Sorensen
Executive Team, Community Church of Joy

Did you catch what Community Church of Joy did? Let me do a bit of highlighting . . .

1. They made a good thing better.

Remember, this was a church of more than 10,000 members. If you keep score by how many cars are in the parking lot, this church was already a clear winner. You'd think they'd just keep doing what they were already doing. It was working.

Except they didn't keep score by counting cars. That number mattered to them, of course, but so did this number: How many people are involved in ministry? Getting people out of the pews and into service helped the church hang onto the new members it was attracting, and it also helped those people grow spiritually.

How are you keeping score at your church? If it's just cars, the impact you're having on your membership is limited. If it's by how many people are involved in ministry, that's another issue altogether. Find out—it's a measurable number that's worth tracking.

2. They acted before they reached a crisis point.

The growth the church expected after the move to a new campus materialized—so it's a good thing they revised their approach to working with volunteers first.

Was it convenient to change their volunteer leadership approach while they were in the middle of planning a relocation? No—but it was important, because how volunteers were able to minister in and through the church was at least as significant a factor in meeting the needs of the unchurched as a new building.

3. They used sound management techniques to get organized.

Do the words "management techniques" bother you? Sometimes in the church world we want to stay as far away from business practices as possible.

Let me suggest this: Call the process you use to work with people anything you want. I prefer "management techniques" because those words describe the process of organizing positions and people fairly well. But it doesn't matter what you call the process—so long as you do it. The Community Church of Joy had some things organized—they didn't have people running around totally unsure what to do. But they couldn't tell how many volunteers they had or precisely what everyone was doing.

Like the Community Church of Joy, you must get organized

or you'll have volunteers uncertain what to do because they don't have volunteer role descriptions. They won't know who they're reporting to, or whether they've done a great job or a poor job. Projects will fail, people will be hurt, and the entire experience will be frustrating for everyone involved.

4. They adopted a process for volunteer leadership that will carry them into the future—no matter how large they grow.

You may be looking forward to seeing an attendance of 100. The idea of 10,000 people showing up is so far into the future you figure it will be your grandchildren who have to sort that out.

But why not put the process in place now that will encourage growth—and that will make sense when your church doubles or triples? It will only be more difficult to institute changes then.

> "What will happen if you *don't* change how you manage the volunteer process at your church?"

What's demanded of many congregations is this: change. And change is frightening in the best of circumstances. And when you're talking about changing church in some way—that's doubly frightening!

But think about it this way: What will happen if you *don't* change how you manage the volunteer process at your church? There are consequences either way, you know—if you act, and if you fail to act.

The unvarnished truth about change is this: It's difficult, often painful, and absolutely essential for the church to deal with if the church intends to remain healthy. Jesus never promised us insulation against change. God may be the same yesterday, today, and forever, but the church must be effective in communicating that unchanging love in quickly changing times. That takes flexibility and an ability to embrace change.

There have been times of stability throughout history, when the amount of change forced on people was minimal. That certainly doesn't describe life today! If life was a lazy, drifting river at one time, we're now hurtling down rapids and bouncing off rocks as we try to navigate quickly enough to stay afloat.

I learned a great deal about how to handle change from— quite literally—a whitewater rapids experience. Let me share what happened with you so I can draw some parallels as to how you can handle change in your church.

Eight Days, Seven Nights

Several years ago I went on an eight-day raft trip down the Grand Canyon. That's the same canyon people point to as an example of how rushing water is so powerful it can slice through rock, slowly carving a chasm more than a mile deep, and stretching as much as 18 miles from rim to rim. Any river that can do that sort of damage—even over an amazingly long time—is nothing to take lightly.

Normally, people like me consider the power of the Colorado River while staring down at it from a safe distance. From the rim of the canyon, the river looks almost picturesque. True, it's cascading down whitewater rapids, splashing a rainbow of spray high over boulders, but there's no danger . . . when you're standing on the rim.

But for eight days I left the safety of the rim and rafted on that whitewater.

The questions I faced about leaving my comfort zone and climbing into a raft are the same questions you have to answer about initiating or improving your volunteer leadership process. Both situations call for handling fast and furious change. And both situations make for one hectic but exhilarating ride.

The first thing you need to do is address your motivation.

To me, roughing it is staying at the Holiday Inn. I love the outdoors, but I'm no adventurer. Lying out under the stars by night and facing whitewater every day was a stretch—a big stretch. So why did I want to go at all?

The answer: My husband, Harvey, and another couple wanted to go, so I thought I'd go along. It was going to be a once-in-a-lifetime experience, and I wanted to share it with my Harvey. I knew there would be whitewater involved and that I was going to have to stretch beyond my comfort level to participate.

When you're looking at initiating change in any organization—the church included—you can assume you're heading into whitewater. What's your motivation? Are you committed enough to see it all through?

Decide where you want to sit as you hit the rapids.

When we found ourselves standing next to the river looking at the raft, I had to decide where to sit. It's not a casual question. When you sit at the front of a raft, you're the first one to make the acquaintance of any boulder you happen to hit, and you're the first person to dive down into the "holes" of swirling water that are everywhere on the river.

If you're in the back of the raft, you'll find yourself lifted high when the raft dives into a hole. And if you're in the middle, you may feel safer, but don't be fooled—you'll be thrown around as the raft rocks and slams down the river.

Harvey and I looked at each other and both nodded. We'd take the front. If we were going to do the trip, we were going to be in for the entire experience. We wanted to sit where we could see what was coming.

As you navigate change in your volunteer program, where are you sitting? Up front is where you get the most warning when something looms in front of you, and that seat gives you the best chance to respond.

Don't back into change. Embrace it and go for it.

Remember to take your sense of humor with you into the whitewater.

I assumed that I'd do lots of screaming and yelling, maybe even some crying. (I *told* you I wasn't an adventurer!) I probably did all of those, but mostly I laughed.

That's right: I laughed. With whitewater cascading all around me, with our inflated raft crashing over rocks, with whirlpools around every turn, I laughed.

When you deal with change, it's essential you bring along your sense of humor. Without the ability to laugh, you're dead in the water. And if you get the chance, surround yourself with other people who know how to laugh, too.

The other couple who rafted with us was the main reason I laughed so hard, so often. My friend Elaine is a five-foot Texas dynamo who's an international consultant in conflict management. She usually looks like she just stepped out of *Vogue* magazine.

Elaine forgot to look at the packing list until the night before leaving for the trip, so the only waterproof jacket she could find was an old, white plastic raincoat that had yellowed and cracked, and that was left from her college days. And her waterproof pants? Fishing waders she borrowed from her six-foot husband. The waders reached her shoulders.

So picture our first morning on the shore. There stood Elaine, looking distinctly *un*-Voguely in her cracked plastic jacket, oversize fishing waders, and a big, floppy hat.

All I could do was burst out laughing.

When we hit whitewater the first time we discovered that you take in *lots* of water on a raft. When we finally reached calm water and stood up to shake ourselves off, Elaine discovered her waders had filled with water. She literally had a geyser of water exploding up out of the waders, and that's a sight I will *never* forget.

Did she get angry? Blame herself or someone else for not having a spare set of waterproof pants on hand? No . . . she laughed.

Find an Elaine when you're heading for whitewater and bring her along. You'll need the humor of friends when you hit the whitewater of change.

Prepare to experience some pain.

With change comes discomfort—and sometimes outright growing pains. But when you step outside your comfort zone, things happen.

For me, the pain started on the third day of the rafting trip. I broke my shoulder. It wasn't an obvious break; we later discovered I had two hairline fractures. All I knew was it *hurt*—and I had a choice to make.

The fourth day of the trip was the last day a helicopter could come in and take me out. If I wanted to get to a hospital, I had to decide to go immediately. If I went further downriver, I was making the entire trip—no matter what.

I decided to stay.

It wasn't a foolhardy decision; it was a decision that the pain I was experiencing was going to be part of the experience. I could handle it—but I *was* forced to make some adjustments.

For instance, I couldn't sit in the front of the raft any longer. I had to move to the back. I couldn't experience the trip precisely as I'd expected, plunging headfirst into the water, but I was still making the trip. And from my new vantage point I saw the entire river differently.

I learned to do things differently, too. I can now dress myself inside a sleeping bag using just one arm. I can't imagine a time that skill will come in useful again, but I've got it. And even better, I know I can adapt. I can be flexible and versatile, and learn something new.

The process of energizing your volunteer process won't go exactly as you've planned, no matter how well you do your planning. Something—or *several* somethings—will happen to impact you. You'll need to learn new skills. You'll need to adapt. And you'll be stronger for the effort.

Stay flexible and versatile. Remember there's seldom one right way to do something. As my colleagues and I present a process for mobilizing volunteers in your church, keep in mind it's a framework. You'll have to adapt it. If you try something and it doesn't work, try something else. Don't get stuck. Don't become negative or obsessed with what fails. Move on.

Never settle for saying, "People are too busy to volunteer." Instead, ask, "How could people volunteer if we structured things differently?"

Decide what you'll focus on—and what you'll let go.

When big organizational change happens, I find a lot of people focus on the "ain't-it-awfuls?" and the "if-onlys," and people get stuck there. They can't let go of what once was or the comfort they once enjoyed.

When I got home from the rafting trip I had to get my shoulder fixed, and that process involved slings, therapy, and painful sessions. But when I think about the rafting trip, I can hardly remember the discomfort. What I recall is the beauty of the canyon, the roar of the water, and laughing until I cried. And I remember a wonderful week with Harvey. I wouldn't have missed it for the world.

One of the challenges for me, living in a changing, white-water world, is remaining an "optimistic pragmatist." By that I mean someone who sees the world realistically. I know there are difficulties that come with experiencing change. I know there are obstacles in the water in front of me. But I choose to remain optimistic as I face those things, confident in a God who's going to be there with me through all of it, come what may.

You get to choose what to focus on, you know. Maybe half of your volunteers deserted the ship when you instituted accountability. Well, what about the half who stayed and flourished, and the new people who were attracted to the volunteer program because it is well-organized now? Focus there.

You could think about the snide comments that came when you changed a process, or you could let those words go, forgiven by choice.

Realize not everyone can tolerate the same amount of change—or risk.

Change involves a certain amount of risk. Maybe nobody will *drown* if the music leader slips an old hymn in among the praise choruses your church has been using for the past few years, but there may be some negative comments. There's risk.

If you're going to initiate change, you need to find people who are willing to go out on the edge with you. Build teams involving those people.

Risk reminds me of another piece of my rafting story . . .

The only other experience I'd had with river rafting was when our son worked as a river guide for two years. Our family joined Rich for a two-day trip, and I'll never forget the first rapids we approached. Rich brought the raft to the shore, got out, and just stood there looking at the river.

I asked him, "What are you doing?" and he said, "I'm reading the river." "Well, why are you doing that?"

Rich said, "Every time we go down the river there are different currents and eddies, and I need to know where they are so we can get through safely."

I assumed Rich had to stop and look because he was a rookie. Experienced guides must certainly be able to handle it as they went, adjusting on the fly.

Only the very best guides lead trips down the Grand Canyon, and our guide frequently got out of the boat, climbed up cliffs, and scanned the river for several minutes before he returned and took us through the rapids.

Taking time to read the river is as important for sunburned old professional guides as it is for first-time rookies.

Guides know there are some principles that *don't* change: how water moves around rocks, what happens when oars are applied to the left side of the raft, how the boat moves through rapids. Those are the same—but the order in which they present themselves can change in the blink of an eye. And there can always be the first time something happens: a huge branch falls in just as the raft passes a cottonwood tree, or the seam on the raft splits.

When you enter the whitewater, change happens . . . sometimes at an alarming rate.

But we serve a God who is changeless in his love for us, and as we seek to involve his children in ministry we're cooperating with his purposes. The three theologies we've discussed are a firm foundation for instituting the process we're outlining. You stand on solid theological ground as change swirls around you.

I suggest that part of your leadership role is to climb up on the high, sturdy cliff of God's love and read the river for your people. You'll be guiding them through the rapids of change, and you want to bring them into places of service and joy safely.

THREE
The Need for Visionary Leadership

Why one person—like you—can make a huge difference.

What will be required of you to put in place a process for volunteer leadership that respects the three theologies we've already discussed? *And* that makes use of the techniques we've learned through years of experience?

Prayer, certainly—because initiating change always needs prayer.

It will take time, too. Don't expect everyone to immediately see the wisdom in the changes you're making. You may well encounter resistance from some of the volunteers and staff, for reasons we'll discuss later in volume 4.

Plan on effort being required. If you don't yet have descriptions of volunteer roles, they'll have to be written. If you don't have a top-notch training and orientation program, it needs to be created. This isn't an easy process, but the results you'll get will make any effort you invest worthwhile.

And you'll also need visionary leadership.

After all the reading, writing, and pondering about leadership I've done over the past 35 years, I believe the definition of leadership I like best comes from Presbyterian pastor and consultant, Mike Murray.

Mike says, "A leader is someone who dreams dreams and has visions, and can communicate those to others in such a way that they of their own free will say 'yes!'"

Here's why I love that definition . . .

Having dreams and visions is not about where you are, but where you want to be. Visionary leadership focuses less on the difficulties of today and more on where we'd be if we somehow got past our difficulties. It's a visionary way of seeing our situations. It's also a faithful way of seeing things.

It sounds easy, doesn't it? So why don't we do more of it in the church?

I think it's because we're so busy doing, surviving, and coping to spend time thinking about the future and where we're heading. When you've got a Sunday school to staff or a sermon to prepare, who has time to dream dreams—even at 2:00 A.M.?

> "A leader is someone who dreams dreams and has visions, and can communicate those to others in such a way that they of their own free will say 'yes!' "
>
> Mike Murray

One of our biggest challenges is to shift our basic paradigms about how we *do* leadership—not how we talk about it. And that takes vision.

One test of a good leader, rather than *How much have I done?* needs instead to be, *How many others have I involved?* This entails *not* doing all the work, but seeing that it's done and done well. This is an enormous shift for church leaders, but a shift that's absolutely crucial! To do it well requires the skills of sound volunteer leadership that we'll explore in detail in this series.

Let me suggest some more *what-ifs* you might want to ask:

What if your pastor's job description changed so the pastor was rewarded for involving others rather than simply getting things done?

What if you asked people to recommend ministry initiatives based on the abilities, skills, and passions they could bring to the table?

What if every leader in your church received training about how to delegate well? You'll learn the fundamentals in volume

3, but realize that it's likely your pastor has never received any training in that specific skill.

Why can I suggest that with some certainty? Because in a recent survey of pastors, Group's Center For Volunteer Solutions discovered that very few pastors had received formal training in working with volunteers . . . or in skills needed to work effectively with volunteers, like delegation.

> **"One test of a good leader needs to be,** *How many others have I involved?"*

That's right: It's possible to receive a post-graduate degree in ministry that does not include even one course in effectively working with volunteers. This in spite of the fact that pastors will spend their entire careers working in volunteer-based organizations.

By the way, if you're reading this book and you happen to have influence in a seminary or two, you have our permission to photocopy this page and send it to whoever you know at those seminaries. Ask why they're setting their graduates up for conflict and failure by not preparing graduates to master the necessary skills to work with volunteers effectively. This Volunteer Leadership Series would make an excellent textbook collection, and there are plenty of additional materials available to create some needed courses.

If we're serious about volunteer ministries thriving, let's prepare our leadership to value and embrace them.

And then there's the rest of Mike Murray's definition of leadership: the ability to "communicate those [dreams and visions] to others in such a way that they of their own free will say 'yes!'"

I love that. It wonderfully sums up the respect leaders need to have for volunteers.

There's no room for coercion when recruiting volunteers. There's no room for manipulation. There's always room for presenting a vision, dream, or mission and letting volunteers who are drawn to it respond with an enthusiastic "yes" that will drive their dedicated service.

> **"The clearer the vision and the more enthusiastically committed to the vision the leaders are, the more likely it is people will catch the vision."**

Here's what I've seen in my many years of working with volunteers: The clearer the vision and the more enthusiastically committed to the vision the leaders are, the more likely it is people will catch the vision. Volunteers have to see, feel, and experience the excitement, and clearly understand how they can help make the dream or vision happen.

When it comes to providing leadership in a volunteer setting, skills of strategy and advocacy are much more important than mere oratory. There are few places where talk is cheaper, or action more necessary.

Let me share a story that illustrates Mike's definition of leadership in action.

Mikey Weiss and 200 Flats of Raspberries

Mikey Weiss retired in 1987 after 40 years in the Los Angeles produce business. One day, Mikey visited his son's produce firm at the L.A. wholesale market just in time to see a forklift hoist 200 flats of raspberries into a dumpster. The fruit was unmarketable, but still edible.

Mikey, watching, had an "aha" moment, and a *what-if* question occurred to him.

Six hundred people were going hungry in a tent city just five miles away. Mikey thought, *What if I could find a way to get produce wholesalers to stop dumping their surplus and instead donate it to organizations that feed the hungry?* That was the day the Los Angeles Charitable Food Distribution Project was born.

Mikey pitched his idea to his produce colleagues, who caught his vision and agreed to help. An extensive volunteer network formed to collect and distribute produce from wholesalers in the area. After hearing about Mikey's efforts, two University of Southern California professors took Mikey's vision even further. They created a model framework of the L.A. project with the goal of helping other cities create similar programs. After all, if it was a good idea in L.A., why wouldn't it be a good idea in Detroit or Des Moines?

Their organization, From the Wholesaler to the Hungry (FWH), has advised and assisted over 38 communities across the country in developing perishable food recovery programs.

One person. One *what-if* moment. One vision. And because of a vision that was communicated clearly and in a way that others could choose to enthusiastically embrace with a "yes," thousands of people were fed.

I ask again, What are your *what-ifs*?

In these turbulent times you can't afford for your church's mission to be fuzzy or out of focus. If you want to inspire volunteers to get behind programs and projects, you'll need to share your vision in a clear, compelling fashion. And you've got to make room in that vision for the participation and ownership of church members.

> "You must make room in your vision for the participation and ownership of church members."

Hang onto that insight: You must make room in your vision for the participation and ownership of church members.

We have a picture of visionary leadership being like Moses coming down the mountainside, carrying tablets etched with the Word of God. Moses wasn't coming to negotiate or to invite commentary. He was there to announce that there was a new law, a new relationship with God. He was proclaiming a vision, and it was up to everyone to get behind it. Period.

But your vision of adding a second service probably doesn't come with that sort of clear-cut, God-given authority. If you want to enlist help making the vision come to pass, you're going to have to be more flexible than Moses was.

The nuts and bolts of turning a vision into a reality reside in the people who carefully craft, plan, and nurture the vision. People like you. People like your church leadership. People like your church membership. This is why I believe volunteer administration is important—I would say absolutely *vital*—in the world and in the church.

After 35 years of working, writing, and consulting in the field of volunteerism, I still fervently believe in volunteerism and the role of managing volunteers. Outstanding, ongoing volunteer participation doesn't just happen; it requires careful nurturing and direction. And it's worth the effort to build excellent volunteer participation.

Why? For many reasons . . .

- Because active participation in ministry often blocks the revolving door that's part of many churches.

In many congregations there are two key numbers that should be measured—but we keep track of just one of them.

The first number represents the number of people who have started attending the church in the past month. The second number represents the number of people who have *quit* attending the church in the past month.

We measure the first number, but often have no accurate idea about the second number. And while we know that people leave and go elsewhere, we don't really know why. There's no reliable mechanism in place to do "exit interviews" to reveal why people chose to leave. They simply disappeared through the revolving door that lets people in and lets people out.

Do this: See what impact getting involved in a ministry position has on the commitment—and longevity—of your membership. Check the numbers. I'm willing to bet that the group of people who have been plugged into appropriate volunteer roles and who are finding meaning in those service opportunities are far likelier to stay—and flourish.

- Because the world needs what the church offers and the good news we proclaim.

These are days that can be discouraging, because even though we know that in the end good will prevail, it certainly doesn't *feel* that way. Not when we see the crime statistics or drive through burned-out, boarded-up neighborhoods.

We can be despairing, believing things will never get better. Or, we can be motivated to reach out, asking God to use us in some small way. Volunteers choose to reach out. They choose hope.

And the world needs all the reaching out and hope it can get.

My friend and colleague Nancy Gaston told me about a woman who phoned her about participating as a volunteer in her church.

> Eileen phoned the Lay Ministry Director with a request. She was recovering from a bout of severe depression and anxiety and was hoping to re-enter the workforce. However, she wasn't sure she had the focus and stamina to work a full day. Was there a job she could do on her own schedule, gradually increasing the daily hours?

> There was. We assigned her the task of cleaning and reorganizing the supply room for the church school program. Coming in daily, she planned the work herself, checking occasionally to make sure her system was acceptable.

> At first she came and went without saying much, but as the daily hours increased, she shared coffee breaks and lunchtime with staff and volunteers—interacting with increasing ease. By the third week, she was working full days and soon completed the task. The supply room looked wonderful, transformed from disorderly piles to organized and brightly labeled shelves.

> We wrote her a letter of thanks and commendation to share with prospective employers, and Eileen started attending worship at the invitation of a volunteer she met over coffee. A month later, she called to say she had a full-time job as a warehouse manager.

> Eileen told us, "I never knew I could organize things like that until you gave me a chance to try it. I feel like a new person—a competent one."

Eileen needed what the church had to offer, and the way she plugged in and got involved was through volunteerism. Imagine the impact that church would have if it was intentional about including outside volunteers in community-based projects like cleaning a park or planting flowers along a public walkway.

We must build relational bridges if we intend to carry the gospel to people. Volunteerism is an excellent way to bring people together.

- Because as we capably manage volunteerism, we create opportunities for people to be at their best as they help others.

My husband's career was in corporate human resources, and I recall one time he turned to me and said, "You're so lucky to be working with volunteers. You get to be with people when they're at their best."

> **"We must build relational bridges if we intend to carry the gospel to people."**

He was right. People *are* at their best when they're so committed to a mission that they set aside their own agendas. When you're stacking sandbags next to a swollen river, standing ankle deep in mud and soaked from a cold, stinging rain, you've got lots of reasons to complain. You're wet and tired. The work is backbreaking. There's no hot coffee. But you and three dozen other Red Cross Disaster Team volunteers are saving a neighborhood, so nobody cares. Moments like that are when people are at their very best in service to others.

Those moments change the lives of people helped, but they change the lives of volunteers, too.

Consider what my friend Stephanie Adams had to say about a volunteer project in which she became involved . . .

> Our church was doing a number of community outreach projects during the Christmas season. This particular project was at the Women In Crisis shelter. Our group went in to do some painting

and cleaning of the shelter. So, the job itself wasn't that special: paint and wallpaper a bathroom. In everyday life that's no big deal.

What affected me was being in the shelter, a place of refuge for so many women who leave home with no possessions, no belongings, often just the clothes on their back. I glanced into rooms that mothers shared with their babies and children. These were women looking for safety and a new start.

After we'd finished for the day, I was relaxing at home when the full impact hit me. There I sat, in my beautiful home, the Christmas tree lit, safe and secure in the knowledge that I was warm and surrounded by love. Blessing and sadness both overwhelmed me.

Blessing, because I knew that God loved me and that everything that I have (and not just the material stuff) comes from him. Yet, at the same time, incredible sadness, because for a part of a day, I was in a place where warmth, love, and security didn't exist for many residents.

Volunteering has never been the same since. Now, whatever I do, it's a grateful response for all the blessings that God has bestowed on me.

- Because it creates new meaning and purpose in people's lives when they discover and use their God-given talents and abilities to make a difference.

A newly divorced woman once walked into the Volunteer Center I founded in Boulder, Colorado. She was new to the area, new to a life without her husband, and she wanted to volunteer at the center. Her realtor had suggested she get to know people by working at the center.

The woman told me she'd had a career as a secretary before getting married 25 years earlier. She said she'd enjoyed it, and I needed a volunteer secretary, so I put her to work.

By the end of her first day, it was clear 25 years away from a typewriter had taken their toll. Every letter she'd typed was filled with errors. I couldn't send out even one of them.

I circled the errors and called her in. "I think these typos slipped past you," I said, and she returned to her desk to re-type the letters. Every one of them.

> "Something amazing happens when we receive time or services from volunteers: We feel worthy."

Here's what happened: She took a typing course and sharpened up those skills. Within a few years she became the supervisor for all the office volunteers. A few years later she was taking on even more responsibility.

Seven years after she walked into the Volunteer Center she left—to become the paid Director of the Big Sisters Program in Boulder. Her time with us turned out to be a seven-year internship that prepared her for a new profession at which she excelled.

- Because involvement in meaningful volunteer efforts can create hope for those who are experiencing life's difficulties.

One of my acquaintances was a volunteer in the Big Brother Program. "It was a life-changing experience for me," Lynn says, "but it had an amazing impact on Brian, my little brother. I couldn't believe what one morning per week did in his life. He and his mom met with social workers all the time, but nothing changed until a guy showed up to take him out for a pizza."

Of course. Think about it from Brian's perspective for a moment. This volunteer set aside Saturdays to spend time with Brian *by choice*. It wasn't the volunteer's job to take Brian fishing, or to talk about school as they kicked through a field looking for arrowheads. No wonder Brian felt special and he listened carefully when the volunteer talked.

Something amazing happens when we receive time or services from volunteers: We feel worthy. We know it's not part of that person's job to help us. It's a gift, and that makes a Saturday morning of time so much more precious. It's not *just* time—it's hope that things will get better.

Nancy Gaston has encountered how God has used volunteer positions to dramatically help the volunteers as well as the people the volunteer is serving.

When Nancy's church distributed a talents and interests survey, one person who responded was a woman named Kelli. Here's what Nancy says about what happened.

> None of us on the Lay Ministry Team knew Kelli—she was a member who seldom attended, wasn't involved, and didn't seem to socialize with other members. Kelli had marked "office support" on her questionnaire—the only item she expressed any interest in.
>
> So the office administrator invited Kelli to come for an interview. She came, but was so shy and withdrawn she didn't even make eye contact. A woman of about 70, Kelli was a recent widow who apparently seldom left her house. She agreed to come in for a half a day per week to do copying and collating.
>
> Gradually, Kelli warmed to the work as well as to the other volunteers and staff. She started to bring snacks to share, and started to show her sly sense of humor. After about six months, she was the person organizing groups to do mailings. She instructed the other volunteers assertively, and looked them in the eye. And after a year or so, she began "seeing" a neighbor who was a widower. They began to attend church together and even stayed for fellowship time—something Kelli had never done before.
>
> And her "gentleman friend" comes along to help in the office on occasion.

- Because when we work together, we create moments and pockets of real community and collaboration.

Visit a Habitat for Humanity worksite and you'll see something you don't often find in the world: a place where titles, roles, gender, color, and age don't matter. Not when everyone is working together for a mission everyone believes in.

You'll often find CEOs swinging hammers alongside teenagers. And when a piece of lumber is hauled past, there may be a successful businessman carrying one end and an economically-challenged single mother carrying the other end. Where else would such a diverse group of people come together to accomplish a task?

Volunteer programs can bring together people who would never get to know each other in any other way. Even in the church, we tend to cluster with our own friends, people who are like us and with whom we have a shared history. Community doesn't automatically happen just because we park in the same parking lot and sit through the same worship service.

But when there's a *what-if* that binds us together, barriers go down. Relationships form. Tasks are shared. Community is experienced.

What you do to encourage volunteerism is important, so it's worth doing well. It's more than simply organizing schedules—it's ministry to those who volunteer, to those whom the volunteers serve, and to the God who pours out talents, abilities, and passions to be used for him.

Let's not settle for "good enough" when it comes to volunteer leadership.

Let's give it our best.

FOUR
Determining If Your Church Culture Is Volunteer-Friendly

Take the temperature of your church to determine if it's volunteer-friendly or volunteer-toxic. Here's a test—and ideas for fixing what needs fixed. Also—the Core Values of Volunteer Leadership!

For more than a quarter century I've lived in a house that sits in the foothills of the Rockies, in the western part of Boulder, Colorado. It's no exaggeration to say that my backyard is in the mountains because my backyard *is* a mountain. I'm halfway up that mountain, so my front yard is a mountain, too.

When I was running a program at the University of Colorado I frequently hosted meetings at my house. Students learned fast that it was always smart to ask where someone lived in Boulder before jumping on a bike to pedal to that address.

If the address was near the University or in eastern Boulder, it was an easy ride on a bike. That part of town is flat.

But if the address was out *my* way, a student could expect a tough, uphill climb. More than once students showed up here looking as if they wished they'd asked a few more questions before heading over to see me.

The good news is that once a person has pedaled uphill this far to a meeting, it's all downhill on the way back!

I don't want to assume that I know exactly where you are as you begin your journey toward launching or improving your volunteer leadership program. Maybe you have a good system in place and it's pretty much easy pedaling for you to get where you need to go.

But maybe it's an uphill climb to get even one person to volunteer for a role at church. You're huffing and puffing and barely making any headway at all. *Anything* would be an improvement over what you're experiencing at your church.

As my colleagues and I write this series of resources to help you create a volunteer-friendly culture, we're aware there are a wide variety of churches in our reading audience. Each of you has your own unique situation, size, history, perspective, and role in the church. Some of you have a long experience working with volunteers, and some of you are new to the field. Some of you are confident, and some of you question God's wisdom in putting you anywhere near the responsibility of helping volunteers find the right fit as they seek to serve in the church.

But one thing you all have in common: *You are the experts where you are.* As we share tools and techniques with you, be open and flexible as you apply them. They must fit the reality of your unique situation to be useful.

For example, if you're a pastor or church leader who's looking for a system to revitalize your whole church's volunteer involvement and you need a centralized function to do it, you'll use the material one way. But if you're the Director of Children's Ministry, Youth Director, Music Minister, or you're concerned primarily with finding volunteers for just one program in your church, you'll use this material differently.

> "Grow toward centralizing the function of volunteer recruitment."

Both are legitimate uses of the volunteer insights and process you'll learn. But I would encourage you to *grow toward centralizing the function of volunteer recruitment.* That's where you'll find the most benefit from putting these tools to use, as Community Church of Joy discovered.

A "Volunteer Manager" or "Volunteer Coordinator" may be the *last* position you can imagine being funded by your church. That position is just now beginning to emerge as a staff function in churches and it's appearing—this is no surprise—first in churches with a large budget and large staff. But it *is* appearing, and I can foresee a day when the "Minister of Volunteer Involvement" is as typical a staff position as "Children's Ministry Director" is today.

Don't believe me? Wait until you see what putting in place a solid, sound process does for volunteer recruitment for your church. In a year see how plugging marginal members into service opportunities builds their commitment and retains them. Do a quick analysis of how many things you once paid to have done are being accomplished by volunteers. As ministry area leaders learn to delegate, see how they are more vibrant—and less burned out.

My prediction is this: In 20 years churches that have *not* centralized the function of volunteer leadership will be the exception. The benefits of doing so are just overwhelming and measurable.

But no matter how you intend to use this material, it's probable you'll run into some obstacles. By discussing them now—before you collide with them—you'll be better prepared to overcome them. It's like pausing to read the river.

It probably won't be terribly helpful to hear this, but you may encounter resistance to launching or expanding your volunteer program that has nothing to do with you. It's not personal. It's cultural.

There are attitudes and behaviors regarding volunteers that are toxic to a healthy volunteer program, and they may have taken root in your church culture decades ago. I've seen the following attitudes and behaviors again and again in churches. Place a check in the box next to any you've seen or experienced in your own church.

Toxic Attitudes and Behaviors

❑ **Committee chairpersons end up doing all the work on their committees.**

This can happen for a number of reasons. It may be that no one ever signed up to serve on the committee, so a single zealot took the project and ran with it. That happens, though it's seldom the best approach.

Another thing that happens is equally bad, if not worse. There *is* a committee, and it may even be comprised of volunteers who want to serve. But because the committee chairperson won't define what needs to be done, or isn't willing or able to share power through delegation, it turns into a one-person show.

For example, suppose Jenny Smith is the newly elected chairperson of the Christian Education Department. She has a new group of committee members sitting around the table in the church hall. It's their first meeting.

Jenny introduces herself and talks about why the project is important, provides information about what's been done in the past, and describes her vision for the future. She covers a remarkable amount of material, hands out printouts, and then closes with prayer.

It's not until the meeting is over that most of the committee members realize that the only person who did any talking was Jenny.

The second meeting comes up on the calendar, and once more the committee sits around a table. And once more they hear Jenny tell everyone what she's accomplished. And once again the members of the committee go home without really needing to be at the meeting. They contributed nothing. They were asked to do nothing.

There's no third meeting.

If you have people in places of power who don't know how to use volunteers, are you willing to provide training?

❑ **A handful of people (the Pillars) do all the work, while the majority of people (the Pewsitters) watch.**

Here's what often happens in churches . . .

The Pillars are those folks who show up for church each week, and who also can be counted on when it's time for the fall festival, the spring father-daughter dance, and the living nativity. They even take a week off work so they can help at vacation Bible school.

Because they *are* so involved, the Pillars have become buddies. And because they're buddies, they usually call each other when it's time to recruit for the next church program. Alisa calls Tricia and says, "Remember when I helped you out on mission weekend? Well, I need your help at the silent auction." They end up creating a club of sorts, one that isn't always open to new members.

Plus, the motivation to participate is often tinged with guilt. Tricia can't very well say no after Alisa housed two missionaries and also made authentic Russian food for the missionary banquet.

It may be that your church's Pillars aren't inclusive of new volunteers. Before you assume that Pewsitters refuse to get involved, find out how effectively Pewsitters are being invited to serve.

And also find out if the Pillars are making all the decisions about church projects and programs. If that's the case, it's no wonder the Pewsitters aren't excited about getting involved. They have no ownership.

❑ **Leaders are asked to cover several major jobs at once—and keep them far too long.**

There are churches that refuse to let someone be in charge of more than one ministry area. Why? Because each ministry area is worthy of having someone focus his or her best energies on it, and because when you stretch people too thin they tend to snap.

Are your leaders burned out? Have they passed the point where their passion sizzles into plain obligation? That didn't happen by accident, and the cause is often overcommitment.

One quick way to be assured you won't have this problem continue is to

> "Are your leaders burned out? Place a time limit on volunteer roles."

place a time limit on volunteer roles. Set a reasonable term for service and make it part of the volunteer ministry description. That way people know how long they're expected to serve, and how to pace themselves. Volunteers can leave the role when their term of service is over, or—if you're both in agreement—they can sign up for another term of service.

Some churches also set a limit on how many terms someone can serve in the same volunteer role. If you have a wonderful small group leader who's serving in an area of talent, skill, and passion, it may make little sense to remove that person simply because some calendar pages have flipped over. But if you have someone who's staked out the nursery as her private kingdom and refuses to make changes or to include others, you'll be glad you have a policy about terms of service.

❏ **Leaders require unrealistic time commitments that scare volunteers away.**

Accepting a volunteer role shouldn't be a life sentence. When we ask potential volunteers to take on open-ended responsibilities ("You'll only be in charge until we find someone else"), we're doing a poor job caring for our volunteers. They know what will happen when they say yes: We'll quit looking for a replacement. We've got them, so why should we continue searching?

There was a time that some volunteers practically lived at the church. These Pillars were the people who thrived on volunteering. But look around: You don't see many of those people around any longer. Because of the trends identified in volume 4, we can't create volunteer positions that are essentially part-time jobs. There must be "entry level" volunteer roles that are episodic or that require few hours.

Review your volunteer job descriptions: Are they so demanding that in a world of two-income families no one can fulfill them? Is either the duration or intensity of volunteer roles unreasonable?

Keep in mind that "unrealistic" is in the eye of the beholder when it comes to time commitments. A major trend in volunteerism is that volunteers prefer three-, six-, or one-month assignments rather than longer commitments. The shorter time commitments fit better into volunteers' busy lives.

❑ **There's no system for coaching volunteers.**

How long would you like to stay in a role where you're not sure you're doing well and there's no feedback? Or if a problem arises you don't know who to call for help? Not long. Yet that's what we do to many volunteers.

Is there a documented process by which you do evaluations of volunteers? If not, you're robbing them of the opportunity to get better in what they do. And that robs the people being served by your volunteers of the chance to be served by ever more excellent volunteers. Check out volume 6 of this Volunteer Leadership Series for more help in creating positive volunteer evaluations.

Plus, there's this: When your wonderful Children's Pastor leaves, will the program disappear with that person? If the pastor isn't developing a second line of leadership, everything ends when the pastor retires, goes to another church, or dies.

Some advice: If you have a program that's working well, *insist* that the leader of that program train others in the nuts and bolts of pulling the program off. You don't want to discover that nothing was ever written down the day after the founder of the program leaves.

❑ **Volunteers are more committed to a leader than to the church.**

Especially if you have a very engaging, inspirational leader, you can have a situation arise in which if the leader leaves, the volunteers leave, too. The volunteers aren't committed to the mission and vision of the church; they're committed to "Pastor Tom."

What draws your volunteers to serve? A relationship with your church's leadership is good—but is it all there is? What are your volunteers' relationship to the mission of the church?

❑ **Clergy and other leaders fail to delegate to volunteers because "It's quicker to do it myself," "I don't want to bother anyone," or "No one does it quite like I do it."**

What's insidious about this obstacle is that probably the staff member who dismisses volunteers as time-consuming is right: It *does* take time to direct volunteers. It *does* take time to bring someone up to speed on a task. It probably *is* quicker to do it yourself—if you want to do it yourself forever.

It's a variation on the old "Give a man a fish and you've fed him for a day; teach him to fish and he'll have food forever" proverb. A volunteer-centered version of that truism might be, "Teach a volunteer to prepare the bulletin inserts and it will take you four hours today. But next week you've got that four hours to go do something else."

Working with volunteers is an investment that will pay dividends—but not immediately. Are your staff and leaders willing to invest in volunteers?

And does your staff truly believe that volunteers *want* to be involved? That it's not a bother to volunteers to use their skills, talents, abilities, and passions in ministry? That it's fulfilling?

And is your staff willing to let loose of *how* a task might be accomplished so long as it's done on time and meets the goal? Frank may *not* design the newsletter quite the same way you would . . . but does it matter? Can you give him a bit of room for creativity and ownership as long as it's clear, accurate, and on time?

Any of these attitudes or behaviors can block your best efforts to involve more congregation members in volunteer ministry roles. Did you place a check in any of the boxes above? If so, you've identified a toxic attitude or behavior you'll need to address.

And I can tell you this: The more boxes you checked, the likelier your church is experiencing a lack of involvement by members and a decreasing membership. And why shouldn't people be drifting away? They're not church "members" in the full sense; they're church "attenders."

I've seen churches that actually *discourage* volunteerism in the congregation. Pastors in those churches would object to that assessment, I'm sure, but it's true. The policies and procedures in place were so toxic to a good volunteer experience that there's no way the majority of church members could participate in a meaningful way.

Every volunteer-toxic attitude or behavior is an obstacle standing between you and where you want to go. If you intend to reach a place where you have a volunteer-friendly church culture, you'll have to go over, under, or around those obstacles—and that takes time and energy you don't have to spare. Plus, getting around them won't solve your problem. What's required is to *remove* those obstacles so the way is clear.

Before tackling the most common obstacles you're likely to face, I'd like to describe the attitudes and actions that typify a *healthy* church volunteer environment. They're summarized in the document you'll find on page 54.

> "I've seen churches that actually *discourage* volunteerism in the congregation."

This set of "Core Values" came out of my sitting in a room for three days with volunteer leadership colleagues whom I treasure as friends. Between us, we had something approaching 250 years of volunteer leadership experience (just think: if we'd been able to put it all together, we could have recruited volunteers for the Boston Tea Party!).

We talked about which principles and "givens" are the foundation of an effective church volunteer program, and we combined those into one document.

The list of Core Values isn't complete—nothing involving volunteer leadership is ever truly the last word. But it's a solid start, and I suggest you copy the document and post it where you'll see it often (for a convenient, abbreviated version see page 111.) It's where you're headed. And if you can, as a church, embrace these principles, you'll find most of the obstacles you're encountering melt away. Couple these principles with the skills and techniques of sound volunteer leadership covered in this series and you'll get where you need to go.

Core Values of Volunteer Leadership

In light of our experience working with volunteers and our own experiences as volunteers, we hold these truths to be truly important—and hopefully self-evident:

Every volunteer experience in the church should encourage a healthy relationship with Jesus Christ.

If that's not a natural outcome of a volunteer experience, either the volunteer has been misplaced in a role or the role isn't one that belongs in the church.

We believe everyone in the body of Christ has something to give to the corporate body.

Volunteer leadership cooperates best with the discipleship and stewardship process by honoring the abilities, interests, and passions of volunteers. We'll take the time to thoroughly interview volunteers and see that they're placed appropriately.

Volunteers are respected as full partners in ministry.

That means we lead volunteers in the same ways we lead paid staff members. Expectations about time may differ, but the standards of behavior and excellence are the same.

Volunteers can be any age.

Adults, teenagers, children—there's room for everyone to volunteer in a meaningful role, doing meaningful ministry.

It's better to leave a volunteer position unfilled than to put the wrong person in the position.

We will place volunteers in accordance to their abilities, interests, and passions, not based on our need to get someone into the junior high boys class.

We provide the resources and training that volunteers need to be successful.

Volunteers can expect to receive careful screening, thorough interviews, accurate job descriptions, and exemplary training and evaluations.

It's okay for potential volunteers to say "no" to a request.

We view a "no" as an invitation to explore alternative opportunities for involvement, not a sign of a potential volunteer's spiritual immaturity.

Volunteer motivation and retention are outcomes of doing other things right.

Among those things are:

• Valuing relationships and celebrating them.

- Valuing experiential training for volunteers.

- Valuing applicable training for volunteers.

- Valuing learner-centered training for volunteers.

- Fostering an environment where there's no put-down humor or victims and where volunteers can count on a culture that's fair, forgiving, and fun.

Volunteer leadership happens best when there's a centralized volunteer leadership function.

Few churches have a designated person handling volunteer leadership. While that's the reality, it's not the ideal situation. We will provide resources to support the *function* of volunteer leadership, yet also encourage the emergence of the volunteer leader *role* in a church setting.

Episodic volunteering is legitimate.

Volunteering in a church setting doesn't have to be an "until death do us part" proposition. We recognize that volunteers may choose to volunteer in one role forever, or switch roles with some frequency. They may be available to volunteer at one stage of their lives and not at another. We'll honor any sort of appropriate volunteering they're prepared and willing to do while fulfilling the needs of the congregation.

We won't let volunteers burn out.

They're too valuable and precious to use up and toss away. We value volunteers serving well over a lifetime more than we value covering tasks.

The good of a local congregation supercedes the good of an individual volunteer.

The desire of a volunteer to serve in a specific area doesn't necessarily mean that's where the volunteer should serve. The corporate good of the congregation comes first in placing volunteers.

And we admit it: We can't motivate volunteers.

Though we can't motivate anyone, we *can* create environments where people experience motivation. Our goal is to "unlock" the innate motivation in individuals as we put in place those values, policies, and procedures that create "volunteer-friendly zones"—places where the culture is fair, fun, forgiving, and faithful. Where truth, trust, and clear expectations pave the way for communication success. Where direct communication is the norm and truth is spoken in love.

Obstacles to a Volunteer-Friendly Culture

The Core Values represent the attitudes and behaviors you want to see in your church. They summarize what a volunteer-friendly culture looks like at a practical level.

Now, what specific things might trip you up as you seek to build an effective volunteer program? Where are the obstacles?

No two churches face precisely the same obstacles. Each church—yours included—is in a unique situation. You may have the issue of having too few people to fill ministry roles. Another church has too many people for one area of ministry, while it's short of people in another area. A church of 50 members has a very different set of challenges than a church of 5,000 members.

You may have a budget that's too small, and another church might have—believe it or not—a budget that's too big. Either can derail a volunteer program.

Let me tell you about a church a colleague of mine visited in Ohio . . .

The Church with Too Much Money

The church building is a majestic stone structure, with steeples making it visible from the entire inner-city neighborhood. The once fashionable streets surrounding the church building have fallen into disrepair over the past 50 years, and what was once a wealthy community has become a needy community. Substantial homes have been divided into apartments and flats. And aside from a few convenience stores tucked into storefronts, merchants have long ago gone out of business or moved to a "safer" neighborhood.

But the church building is immaculate. Every brick has been scrubbed clean of gang graffiti, and an armed guard patrols the perimeter each night. The parking lot is freshly sealed, and not one pane of glass is broken or covered with wire.

It's as if the church property has been frozen in time. It may be a depressing, decaying new millennium outside the church fence, but inside it's 1951.

When my friend went into the building for a tour, he was greeted by an associate pastor who proudly showed him through the facility.

The sanctuary, which seated more than a thousand in carved wooden pews, smelled of fresh wood wax. The Christian education wing held more than a dozen classrooms, each with tiny tables and chairs in perfect rows. The nursery was spacious and newly carpeted.

All for a congregation of 32 people, with an average age of 67.

The associate pastor explained that on Sunday mornings the congregation enjoyed tremendous choral music—students from the nearby university's College of Music were under contract to sing and play. And another student was hired to sit in the nursery, on call to take care of any baby whose family came to visit.

No baby had been in the nursery for more than two years.

And the classrooms? Each week they were dusted and cleaned, but there was no Christian education program because there were no children—they'd graduated the last child out of the children's ministry department 15 years earlier.

What kept the doors open? An endowment funded by bequests in wills guaranteed that the building would always be kept in tip-top shape. The halls might echo when a visitor walked through on Sunday morning, but the halls were always perfectly waxed.

The church knew it was in trouble. It needed to attract visitors, preferably from the neighborhood, so my colleague was asked to make that happen. He'd be well-paid to put together community events that would bring people into the building, and hopefully into the church.

But because of their advanced age and busy schedule, none of the church staff or members of the congregation expected to be involved. My colleague could hire help as he saw fit from temp agencies, or through the university student union office.

My friend refused the assignment.

A huge budget had choked off volunteer involvement in this church because they could afford to pay others to do everything. In this case, too much money was a bad thing.

"A huge budget had choked off volunteer involvement in this church because they could afford to pay others to do everything."

Assuming a bottomless budget isn't an obstacle in your way, what *are* the obstacles you're facing?

I've observed that obstacles tend to fall into one of three categories:

1. Staff members who resist volunteer involvement,

2. Volunteers who resist serving, and

3. Inadequate volunteer leadership.

Let's look at these one at a time, and how we can approach overcoming them.

Why Staff Members Resist Volunteer Involvement

• Leaders have had a poor experience with volunteers.

The volunteers were late. They didn't do what they were asked to do. They didn't follow the rules. They were more interested in talking with each other than in finishing the work. The list of what constitutes a "poor experience" goes on and on.

The obvious questions to ask would be what happened and whether it was specific to a particular volunteer or it was caused by the design of the role a volunteer was filling.

And what might keep the experience from being repeated?

Work through the issues with leaders and encourage them to approach future volunteer encounters with an open mind. If a leader simply won't work with volunteers, don't place volunteers with that leader. Let the success of the program in other ministry areas slowly change the leader's opinion of volunteers.

• Leaders fear they'll lose their positions.

There *is* something awkward about having a former administrative assistant from a successful business helping out a church secretary who isn't a stellar administrator. Sometimes volunteers do a job so well that people begin to joke that the leader being helped isn't really needed anymore. Everyone laughs—except the leader.

An insecure leader can create tremendous problems for volunteers, so discuss with leaders the benefits of using volunteers. The leader will be able to actually grow in his or her position because some tasks that formerly required attention will be handled by volunteers. Help the leader see the involvement of volunteers as an opportunity, not a threat. Assure leaders that volunteers will report *to* them, and aren't being brought in to replace them.

• Leaders fear the volunteers will make them look bad.

Perhaps it's fear that a retired principal who wants to help with the children's ministry will question decisions made by the children's pastor. Or that a board member who's helping with the ushering will tell the board that ushers really aren't needed, and the group should be disbanded.

Encourage these leaders to welcome input from volunteers, and to think of them as full partners in ministry. Encourage volunteers to be sensitive to the roles of their leaders, and to support those leaders.

• Leaders fear volunteers are unreliable.

This is a realistic fear—some volunteers *are* unreliable. Share with leaders the screening, training, and orientation you'll be doing with volunteers. Ask that the leader give volunteers a chance—and do your best to place reliable people in that leader's area.

• Leaders want to recruit their own volunteers.

This is the system at place in many churches—each ministry area is responsible for its own staffing. In many respects, the system works well. An area ministry leader has a good understanding of the sort of person who will fit and be successful.

In a centralized system of volunteer leadership, it's *still* the leader of a ministry area who does the final interview and determines if a volunteer will be placed in that area.

But there's a potential problem when each ministry does its own recruiting. Some leaders just aren't very good at recruiting, and they're perpetually short of volunteers when another ministry area is abundantly staffed. And if the children's pastor is recruiting just for only her ministry area, she may not know about positions in youth ministry or the choir. Her filter for who will make a "good volunteer" is someone who fits in the children's ministry area.

Unfortunately, this approach sabotages the overall volunteer program and builds resentments in areas where leaders aren't able to recruit effectively. Assure leaders that no volunteer will be placed in his or her area without that position being offered by the leader. No leader will be "stuck" with someone.

- Leaders don't want to bother with supervising volunteers or completing the necessary job descriptions.

Unfortunately, both responsibilities come with having volunteers involved. If a leader refuses, politely offer to help create the job descriptions and to provide training for the volunteers. If the leader still refuses, don't place volunteers with that leader. Let the success of the program in other ministry areas influence this leader. Encourage peers who are using volunteers successfully to share their stories with this leader.

- Leaders believe that using volunteers creates more work than it's worth, and they aren't rewarded for using volunteers.

Two issues are reflected here: the cost to leaders of supervising volunteers and the importance of volunteers being in ministry.

Discuss with leaders that it's *worth* paying a price to involve people in ministry. In the same way it's important to let children "help" at tasks until they master them, it's worth helping volunteers master tasks. Why? Because then the body of Christ has fully-functioning members who are serving others and glorifying God in service. Encouraging that is one of the primary responsibilities of leadership in the church. Working with volunteers needs to be seen as a primary part of the leaderships' responsibility and rewarded as such.

Do this to get a discussion going: Suggest that working with volunteers become a part of each staff member's job description for the reasons discussed above.

Staff objections to volunteer involvement fall into two general arguments: those borne out of experience and those fueled by fear.

If a staff member has truly had a negative volunteer experience, explore it in detail. Help the staff member determine how much of the problem was due to the volunteer, and how much was contributed by the staff member. What safeguards do you have in place—or *will* you have in place—to keep the same sort of situation from developing again? Sometimes just your continued involvement to monitor the staff member/volunteer role fit is enough to gain support.

But realize this: You can't *force* a volunteer on a staff member. If a specific staff member refuses to work with volunteers, that's a reality of your world. Work with the staff members who are willing to work with you, and encourage *them* to do the work you can't do: changing the hearts and minds of their peers.

Why Volunteers Resist Serving

Why do people refuse to become actively involved? Why do Pewsitters decide that a life of disengagement—which is boring and not consistent with their purpose in the church—is preferable to finding a place to serve? Again, the obstacles are numerous, but in my experience here are the most common obstacles you'll need to overcome:

• "There aren't any jobs I can do."

When your potential volunteers see programs being delivered with excellence, the potential volunteers tend to focus on their own limitations. They see outstanding musicians leading singing, top-notch teachers doing children's ministry, smiling ushers greeting everyone like long-lost friends—it's daunting.

Communicate to potential volunteers that there's training for any role they think suits them, and that you'll only place volunteers where they have God-given strengths.

- "I filled out one of those time and talent sheets and nobody called me."

All too often churches collect information about members and then promptly do . . . nothing. As you'll see in volume 4, the volunteer interview process tightens up that loop and removes the possibility of inaction.

What you don't want is to let a time and talent sheet officially reject people's gifts once a year. At a workshop I was leading, a lovely, silver-haired lady told me this sad story:

"My husband passed away, so I moved here about a year and a half ago to live with my daughter. One of the first things I did was join a church. When I joined, they asked me to fill out a form listing my interests and talents and how I'd be willing to serve. I wrote down a long list because I was very active in my old congregation and now had lots of time on my hands. I was also eager to feel like I belonged in my new church family. It's been a year and a half and nobody has ever called to ask me to do anything. It makes me very sad."

Filling out paperwork doesn't place potential volunteers in fulfilling positions. We do that. Whatever paperwork we use is just a tiny first step in the process.

- "I was so frustrated last time that I'll never volunteer again."

Here's a dirty little secret: Many of those "frozen chosen" Pewsitters *have* been volunteers in the past. They didn't quit because they got too busy, or too old, or too anything. People don't easily quit things they find personally rewarding.

They quit because they were in poorly defined roles, and they lacked the resources or authority to be successful. The problem wasn't with the volunteers—it was with the system in which they volunteered.

Again—a volunteer interview program eliminates most of the opportunity for frustration because before a position is offered to a volunteer, that position has a job description in place, as well as a structure that provides evaluation and support.

- "I hated my volunteer job."

Bad volunteer experiences happen to good people for a variety of reasons. Sometimes it's the fault of the volunteer— he or she isn't really committed, or isn't able to give the time and energy the role requires. If the volunteer misrepresented what he or she was willing or able to do, that's going to create tension and failure.

But sometimes the problem was that the volunteer was dumped on by a leader. By that I mean the task given wasn't really delegated, it was dumped.

The difference is this: If a leader thoughtfully thinks through how to share his or her work and hands off a task with the necessary resources and authority—that's delegation. If the task is something the leader *meant* to do but ran out of time and then in desperation handed it off—that's dumping.

Nobody likes to be dumped on . . . and few people will stick around to have it happen twice. When a volunteer has been delegated a task, that allows the volunteer to do ministry. But when a task has been dumped—that feels like anything *but* doing ministry.

And sometimes volunteers disliked the roles they were in because they were in the wrong role all along. The volunteer soldiered along either until the results were so poor the volunteer was asked to leave, or he or she was so miserable he or she quit.

The volunteer interview program offers the best opportunity to make a good fit for each volunteer, to get each person into the right job.

- "Nobody seemed to care about me—or my ideas."

Church leaders need to admit it: Sometimes we've made filling jobs the goal, not placing the right person in the right job. We're handed a list of sixteen slots to fill on the organizational chart, and that's our focus. As long as someone is willing to let us write down his name, that's good enough for us.

Then we're off to fill the next chart.

There's no training. No follow-up. No evaluation. Little communication.

Who wants to work in a place like that—especially since volunteers don't have to do it? Sooner or later, people leave, and they're not inclined to come back. We haven't communicated that we care about people.

And when it comes to caring about people's ideas, there are two things we should never, ever say: "We don't do it like that here," and "But this is the way we always do it here." Those are two of the most demotivating phrases we can utter.

The message with either phrase (and attitude) is that we don't need your ideas, that we're happy with the status quo.

Here's what I've found: Volunteers don't care whether you actually implement their ideas. They're happy when you do, of course, but it's not essential. What *is* essential is that you actually *hear* the volunteer's idea and communicate respect for the idea and the volunteer who suggests it.

- "I don't have time."

We'll deal more with this in the context of recruiting in volume 4, but let me quickly respond to this obstacle now.

We all have the same amount of time in a day, a week, and a year. The issue isn't a lack of time, but that the volunteer opportunity being presented isn't important enough to rate a time commitment. We all make time for what we value most.

Never be put off by the claim that there's "no time" for volunteering. There is. The true issue is something else.

- "I feel awkward talking about myself."

Under the best of circumstances, it's difficult for church members to tell us what they can do and what they can't do. It feels like bragging to point out one's strengths, and few people like to admit to weaknesses.

So potential volunteers wistfully wish they could be given a role that actually fits them—but it's never offered. And it's never offered because we don't know to offer it. Instead, we offer roles that volunteers either try and hate, or wisely refuse to take at all.

It's also hard for church members to tell us what they're *tired* of doing. That feels like giving up, or not being faithful. Here's a story that illustrates this point . . .

An acquaintance of mine joined a church and volunteered to help out in the Sunday school. She had a strong background working with junior-highers, so she was asked if she'd teach that age level. She agreed, and one Sunday morning she was walked up the stairs to where that class met.

Here's what she saw as she came through the door: a tired man reading aloud from the book of Judges. He'd been working his way through the Old Testament, reading it aloud, as his three students suffered along.

One student was busy scratching the varnish off the table with his fingernail. Judging from the almost total lack of varnish left, he'd been at it awhile.

The second student was gazing out a window.

The third student was sound asleep.

The new teacher was introduced, and the man leading the class looked up in surprise. He shook her hand, closed his Bible, and walked out the door without saying a word.

It wasn't until later that my acquaintance found out the man had asked three years earlier if he could be relieved of duty. He didn't want to teach junior-highers any longer; he wanted to transport elderly people to church from nursing homes. *That's* where his passion was.

And the boy who was sleeping? That was the man's son.

A final thing we fail to hear from volunteers: what they would like to learn. What skills they'd like to develop. What talents they want to explore. Those places are where their interests lie—but we never get to tap into that fountain of motivation and enthusiasm. Why? Because we don't directly ask.

Why Inadequate Volunteer Leadership Can Be an Obstacle

This last category of obstacles is all about us—the leadership and management issues *we* bring into the equation.

Nobody wants to rearrange deck chairs on a sinking ship. It's

Why Do You Call These People "Volunteers"?

Perhaps it's not appropriate to call someone who is supposed to serve (remember our three theologies: *everyone* is called into significant ministry) a "volunteer," but that's the term we've chosen to use.

Some churches use other words to describe people who fill roles in the church. "Minister" and "servant" are among terms that some churches feel more accurately describe a Christian's role, considering that all believers are instructed to make available their God-given abilities, skills, and passions for service in the body of Christ.

Our research has shown, though, that only the word "volunteer" was widely recognized by most people in a congregation. An announcement asking for "ministers" to participate in a service role may leave some lay people thinking that only those with seminary degrees need apply.

If you do choose to avoid the word "volunteer," consider simply referring to all people in volunteer roles as " unpaid staff." A Sunday school teacher would be a children's ministry unpaid staff member; a parking lot attendant would be a hospitality ministry unpaid staff member.

The word "staff" signals that every role is valuable, and invites volunteers to think of their work as meaningful and on a par with pastoral staff and other paid individuals. It respects their full significance in ministry, but again—it may create confusion in the minds of potential volunteers.

meaningless. When a ship is floundering, what people want most is to find a way off the ship. Everything else is busywork.

What's the reputation of your church when it comes to volunteers? Are you perceived as a sinking ship or a ship that's sailing along toward important places? When you run your mission up the center mast, do people salute?

When we ask volunteers to do things that aren't central to

the mission of our church, we're providing inadequate leadership. When we ask volunteers to sign up for roles without giving them the information they need, we're providing inadequate leadership. And when we put volunteers in roles that don't suit them, we shortchange volunteers. It's easy to commit each of those sins, and each sin helps sink our reputation.

The fact is, we can be our own worst enemies when it comes to working with volunteers. What we say, what we do—in spite of our best intentions, we can easily create systems that make getting and keeping volunteers difficult.

That's why I'm so excited that you're working through this series of books on volunteer leadership. You're clearly ready and willing to do your best to create a culture and structure where it's easy for people to embrace their God-given abilities, skills, and passions, and use those in ministry.

None of us will ever be a perfect volunteer leader any more than we'll ever be a perfect follower of Christ. There will always be room for improvement and growth.

But you're growing—and God will bless and multiply your growth.

Let's look at three obstacles we may be throwing in our own way . . .

- "I'll do it alone."

If you feel like a lonely voice crying in the wilderness, you're in trouble for two reasons. First, you're in the wilderness. You won't get much done there.

Second, nobody is listening to you. You're alone.

If you're the sole owner of the volunteer program in your church, the first thing you need to do isn't recruiting volunteers to fill the bell choir. The first thing you need to do is recruit people who'll share your vision and be your co-laborers.

You *cannot* run a volunteer program alone. It's too challenging and time-consuming. The work is never done. The phone calls never end. You must find some help. A team will provide you not just extra hands and feet, but also morale-building and fellowship.

If you're a person who thinks you've got to do it yourself to get it right, think again. Practice what you're preaching and recruit a team . . . even if you don't think you need one. *Especially* if you think you don't need one!

• "I'm relying on spiritual inventories."

Perhaps you've tried to determine where your congregation is concerning volunteer ministry by using a spiritual gifts inventory. I applaud you if using a gifts inventory, or a time/talent survey, has actually increased your membership's level of service and involvement.

Frankly, that's often not the case.

In many churches where inventories are administered, they don't result in the actual placement of people in meaningful ministries. Why? Because there's no system of volunteer leadership to connect people with volunteer roles. Too often church members are left frustrated as they think, *Now I know the name of my spiritual gift—but what do I do with it?*

If you want to use spiritual inventories and surveys, wonderful . . . but here are some shortcomings that tend to create issues:

They're based on self-reporting. People describe what they're like, and that often provides a skewed view of their skills and abilities. We often see ourselves as more or less gifted than we really are. Sometimes we don't have a realistic view of our own abilities at all.

One way to remove this shortcoming is for each person who completes an inventory to have three or four close friends complete the same inventory *about* that person. It greatly increases the amount of work involved, but you'll get a clearer view of the person. If Brian sees himself as a gifted administrator but his wife and two friends see just the opposite—that's good to know.

Churches don't act on information gathered. One church went to the expense and trouble of having every adult member complete a survey. The surveys were forwarded to the church office where they were carefully tabulated, collated, and filed away. When volunteer roles opened up in the church the leaders of those volunteer ministries skimmed through the surveys looking for a match.

The problem was that people who were interested in volunteering had already done so—and not necessarily within the church. The local Habitat for Humanity and Salvation Army offices received lots of volunteers after the survey was given. Why? Because after several months passed without hearing from the church leadership, potential volunteers assumed that they weren't needed at church—so they looked elsewhere.

If you've ever offered a personal gift to someone who unwrapped it, yawned, and tossed it aside, you know how it feels to fill out a time and talent sheet and have nothing happen as a result. It's a systematic rejection process.

Let me tell you about a friend I'll call Audrey Ferris. Her experience isn't uncommon.

Audrey was new to her church, St. Peter's, and didn't yet feel fully comfortable or accepted. It's not all the fault of the church—Audrey is a shy person who likes to be part of things, but doesn't always know how to go about joining in. So by temperament she was stuck a little on the outside, but wanting in.

Then, one day a letter came. The Stewardship Committee had sent out the annual form, and Audrey was in a quandary. Deciding how much money to give was no problem, but she agonized over the time and talent portion of the form. Did she have time to share? Yes . . . but she wasn't sure she had any talent.

But she wanted to give more than money—by signing up to serve in a ministry area she'd get involved, become part of the group. She'd be known and accepted.

Audrey lay awake for hours agonizing over what boxes to check. What if she tried something and failed? What if she checked the wrong box? What if she really didn't have any talents?

In the morning she reviewed the list again, and after prayer and nail-biting she checked two boxes: typing in the office and helping with kindergarten in Sunday school. She felt a small thrill of anticipation as she tucked the list in her Bible, and an even larger thrill when the next Sunday she laid her form on the altar.

Stewardship Sunday had come, and at last she'd stepped forward to volunteer.

She waited for the phone to ring. She waited . . . and waited . . .

She's waiting still, and two more Stewardship Sundays have come and gone. She no longer places an "X" in any of the boxes.

Even if you act on information given, we strongly urge you to do one-on-one interviews with church members. You'll discover a wealth of information that you won't find in any other way.

There's no personal interview to discover deeper information. Okay, so a potential volunteer is a talented professional musician. The volunteer has received tremendous ovations time and again. Music is a passion, a talent, and, as far as the potential volunteer is concerned, a curse. After 20 years of playing music non-stop, the person would rather do *anything* than play one more note.

A gift inventory might well indicate that this person would make a perfect worship leader, and were the volunteer's attitude different that's true. But the test won't reveal that the volunteer will take any other role before being condemned to do on Sunday what he does every other day.

Interviews reveal attitude, interest, and enthusiasm. You'll find out how to do effective interviews in volume 4. Don't skip this step—it's a powerful tool in placing volunteers where they'll thrive.

• "I'll get through this crisis, then start to do it right."

Think this and you'll just stay on the treadmill for another round.

Let's say someone hands you a list of "church jobs" to fill so programs can keep running. Maybe you've got a shopping list of three ushers, two committee heads, and a choir director. You fill those slots with willing people, but now you've got another five people who may be in the wrong roles. You haven't got the foggiest notion if they're going to thrive in their new jobs, or wither and die there.

There's no end to crises if you've got people in the wrong jobs. It's like being in the eye of a hurricane: You can walk outside to see how bad the damage is and what's still standing, but you know the second half of the storm is coming. There's always another crisis on the way.

Let me suggest this: If you haven't got time to do proper volunteer placement now, you'll never have time. That's because you're creating future disgruntled volunteers, unhappy volunteer managers, and an environment that's toxic for volunteerism.

Your intentions may be good—but your actions aren't. You're not following a key concept of volunteer leadership: *People are every bit as important as programs.* That sounds simple, but it has some huge implications, such as:

We won't sacrifice people so programs can continue. If there aren't enough volunteers to staff the nursery properly, we declare the nursery off-limits until we have sufficient volunteers in place. That may sound radical, but think of what will happen if you have two haggard volunteers caring for 23 infants. Not only is it unsafe, but you'll lose the two volunteers you have.

We won't think of "volunteers" as a unit, but as a collection of unique individuals. If you don't know the names of volunteers who serve in your ministry area, how will you help them feel welcome? How will you know how to thank them? How will you be able to help them grow in their service? May the words "Let's leave that to the volunteers" never again be spoken in your church. Rather, let us hear words like "That sounds like something Frank, Tim, and Lenora would do well."

Programs—even long-standing ones—may for a time be discontinued. If you think starting a church program is hard, try stopping one that's become a tradition. It will seem like you're pulling the life-support plug on a loved one. But if there aren't enough organ-playing volunteers who stand ready to maintain and play the pipe organ, maybe it's time to give it up, at least for a while.

In the following survey let me quickly summarize the attitudes and behaviors we've identified as contributing to a toxic environment for volunteerism:

Attitude and Behavior Survey

Check each box you think applies to our church as you experience it. Please check boxes on the basis of what we *actually* appear to believe and do, not what we *should* believe and do.

❑ Leaders don't truly believe that God has called each believer to do significant ministry.

❑ Leaders don't truly believe each believer has a God-given ability, skill, or passion to use in ministry.

❑ Leaders don't truly believe that each believer has a place where he or she fits into the body of Christ.

❑ Committee chairpersons end up doing almost all the work on their committees.

❑ A handful of people (the church Pillars) do most of the work while others (the Pewsitters) watch.

❑ Leaders are asked to cover several major jobs at once—and keep those jobs too long.

❑ Leaders require unrealistic time commitments that scare volunteers away.

❑ There's no organized system for coaching volunteers.

❑ Volunteers are more committed to a leader than to the church.

❑ Clergy and other leaders fail to delegate to volunteers.

❑ Leaders are hesitant to work with volunteers because of a poor experience in the past.

❑ Leaders fear they'll lose their positions.

❑ Leaders fear the volunteers will make them look bad.

❑ Leaders think volunteers are unreliable.

❑ Leaders want to pick their own volunteers.

❑ Leaders don't want to bother with supervising volunteers or completing the necessary job descriptions.

❏ Leaders believe that using volunteers creates more work than it's worth and that they aren't rewarded for using volunteers.

❏ Volunteers don't think there are jobs they can do adequately.

❏ The church doesn't follow up on spiritual gift inventories or time and talent sheets.

❏ Frustrating volunteer experiences aren't debriefed and resolved.

❏ Volunteers have been placed in inappropriate jobs.

❏ The church is perceived as unresponsive to volunteers' suggestions.

❏ Volunteers feel uncomfortable talking about themselves at our church.

❏ Ministry leaders prefer to accomplish tasks on their own.

❏ It's perceived as too big a challenge to change the existing system of volunteer placement—even if it's inadequate.

What are other attitudes and behaviors that affect volunteers and volunteerism in our church but aren't noted above? Jot them in below:

❏ _____

❏ _____

❏ _____

❏ _____

I am: a paid church staff member_____ a volunteer_____

Now glance at the boxes you and others have checked. Those are your prayer list. Ask God to work in the hearts of his people to change those attitudes and behaviors and to give you patience as you identify and deal with those attitudes and behaviors in others.

Also, pray that God uses you to help his people find appropriate places of service and experience joy in serving. You'll be cooperating with God's purposes as you assist in this ministry—may you find joy, too!

You know where you are—there are strengths in your church and weaknesses when it comes to volunteerism and the use of volunteers.

But where are you going? What's your destination?

May I suggest this? You want—you *need*—a Volunteer Leadership System built on solid biblical theology and solid volunteer leadership principles. Your next step is to catch a vision for a future that has that system in place.

FIVE
Defining Your Future

Use this 12-step process for getting you where you want to be: enjoying a healthy, vibrant volunteer program that places the right people in the right jobs, and serves everyone involved.

Okay, we've established that your church has some room for growth when it comes to encouraging volunteerism. That means you're just like every other church I've encountered in 35 years of consulting, including my own congregation. I've yet to see a church that doesn't have room for growth.

So what are you going to do about it?

Let me begin by saying this: *No matter what obstacles you face, they can be overcome.* Don't be discouraged. I didn't ask you to identify the challenges you face so they could stop you. I asked you to take a clear, realistic look at those challenges so you'll know how to proceed as you move forward.

In this chapter I'm going to outline a process that will be further developed as you read through this Volunteer Leadership Series. I'll briefly comment on the steps of the process so you can determine where you are at present and so you know what to do next.

But two cautions:

1. It's important you not skip steps. You may have to adapt some of the steps to fit your situation (remember: *you're* the expert in your situation!), but each step has a definite purpose. It's like baking a cake: You can skip an ingredient as you mix the batter and at first it won't show, but once you've cooked the cake it will be obvious from the results that something was missing. This process is your recipe for volunteer leadership success. Don't skip any ingredients!

2. It's important you take these steps in order. You can't jump right to placing volunteers (step #8) before you set objectives and goals (step #3). This is a linear process, and each step builds on those before it. Like the Core Values, I suggest you make a copy of this process (a summary is on page 89) so you can refer to it often. Hang it next to the Core Values list so you'll have a description of the culture you want to see created and the process by which you'll accomplish the following:

- You'll mobilize and energize more volunteers.

- You'll stop clergy and lay-leader burnout.

- You'll get the right people in the right jobs.

- You'll develop future leaders through effective delegation.

- You'll create a volunteer organization that's always being renewed and reinvented to stay current with trends that impact volunteerism in your community.

If that's the future you envision, let's get started!

The Volunteer Leadership System: 12 Steps

I've used the Volunteer Leadership System in hundreds of voluntary organizations and churches. It's a centralized volunteer leadership system that brings about a "heart transplant" in organizations. That is, once it's in place it engenders a culture that's open to volunteers, and it encourages volunteers to grow in their service.

I'll walk you through the steps in order.

Step 1: Establish a Vision

A vision answers the questions, "Where are we going?" and "Where does God want us to be in five years?"

It's determining what we'd like our future to look like. We can just limp along hoping everything will work out, but that's neither proactive or powerful. Volunteers don't rally around the call of "Well, let's hope things don't get any worse."

Here's the truth: Without vision the people perish . . . and without vision a local *church* perishes, too.

Not everyone is good at imagining the future and seeing where God is taking them. Not everyone is good at implementing things, either, or maintaining systems. Visioning requires a blend of skill, faith, and faithfulness to keep the vision grounded.

There often isn't anything terribly mystical about envisioning the future; it's doing some level-headed thinking about what truly is happening and what the implications are. Here's an example of how that can pay off for an organization . . .

My friend John was delighted to discover, on a long airplane flight, that he was seated next to the Chief Planner of McDonald's. Since at the time John was the director of Colorado University's Graduate School of Business Management, he couldn't believe his luck. What a great opportunity to uncover some top-notch business techniques! John asked if he could pump the Chief Planner for insights to share with students, and the man agreed.

"But," warned the Chief Planner, "I'm not sure you'll believe how we do it."

John insisted anyway, and he quickly pulled out a pen so he could take notes on how one of the world's fastest-growing international companies did planning that carried them into the future.

The Chief Planner revealed that at the top of the McDonald's corporate headquarters in Chicago there was a special planning room. In the room was a skylight, a waterbed, and nothing else.

"Every department manager is required to spend one hour per week up there alone," said the Chief Planner. "The manager has to be on the waterbed, looking out the skylight. As the head of planning, I'm required to spend one hour per *day* up there. It's in my job description."

The Chief Planner continued, saying it was when he was on that bed, staring out the skylight, that the implications of zero population growth really hit him. This conversation took place during the years when the U.S. birthrate had declined and grade schools were being closed almost daily.

At that time McDonald's entire ad campaign was Ronald McDonald selling burgers and fries, and it was aimed squarely at kids. "We've got an entire planning department," the Chief Planner admitted, "and the population statistics were around . . . but nobody had put those statistics together with our future."

It was at that moment, on that bed, that McDonald's breakfasts were born. An entire diversification aimed not at children, but at adults.

You've got statistics, too. You know what's happening in your church and in your community. But have you put those together? Have you invited God to help you apply your creativity to the future—to take what the statistics tell you and to determine how you'll navigate those realities? To read a statistic and then ask "so what?" and "what if?"

You need a vision for your church and your ministry. Begin with the church's vision, because the volunteer leadership vision must support that larger corporate vision.

In volume 2 we'll focus more on identifying and communicating a vision for your volunteer leadership program.

Step 2: Write Mission and Purpose Statements

Here's where you establish what business you're in—what problems you're trying to solve. If your mission is to present the Gospel to each person in your town, that's going to drive some of your decisions. It means you'll quickly fund an outreach in your community, but you might think twice about helping establish a seminary overseas.

If you're creating a mission or purpose statement for only your ministry area, you'll focus on how you can do children's ministry, youth ministry, or hospitality in such a way that you help the corporate church achieve its mission and purpose.

Start with your church's mission and purpose statements and be sure you support those. And if there aren't any corporate statements, encourage the church leadership to create them. The outline below will help them—or you—get started. So will the further discussion of mission statements found in volume 2.

What is God calling you to be in this time and this place? The answer today as you're a church of 100 may change when you're a church of 1,000. As your neighborhood becomes more urban, or suburban, your mission may change. What's important is that you're deliberate and prayerful about stating it clearly.

Step 3: Set Objectives and Goals

In volume 4 of this Volunteer Leadership Series there's a discussion of how to create goals for marketing your program. The elements of a goal are discussed in detail there, but here's a quick summary.

How to Create a Mission Statement

1. Get the right people involved. Anyone who has a stake in the outcome should be involved in the process.

2. State WHY you exist—your purpose and what you want to accomplish. Keep the statement simple, and be honest and direct. Flowery prose has no place; you're writing to inform, not inspire.

3. Define WHO you want to serve. Who's your audience? Who should be paying attention to you?

4. Outline HOW and WHERE you'll get it done. Are you delivering goods and services? working with a specific group of people or in a specific location? Say so.

5. Remember your mission statement isn't being carved in granite. It will change as your organization changes.

To be useful, a goal must be written clearly and simply, and it must be specific. What *exactly* do you want to accomplish? Until you're specific, you can't determine if you've met the goal.

Make goals attainable. It doesn't do anyone any good if your goal is so lofty that nobody believes it can be reached. Who wants to give their best efforts to stretch for a goal that won't be reached anyway?

Make goals measurable every way possible, too. By time, certainly—decide when something needs to happen and put a calendar date on it—and also by number. If you need to schedule 12 appointments each month to place 6 volunteers, then create a goal of scheduling 12 appointments each month.

It's human nature for some of us to shy away from goals. We don't want to be locked in or fail to meet the goals. In the same way some sales professionals find goals motivating, some people find that goals suck the joy out of a task. Besides, when we're talking about "church stuff," how do you set a goal? When you tell God you want to see ten new children join the Sunday school, isn't that stepping over a line?

Forgive me, but I don't see setting goals as telling God what to do or failing to live faithfully. Setting goals is about focusing your energy and putting on paper what you trust God will do to and through you. You already know the goals you set are in accordance with what you've determined God wants to do in your church because your goals have flowed out of your mission. Why *not* be specific about what you're trusting God to accomplish?

Step 4: Write an Action Plan

Action plans are where you determine what steps will get you to each goal. Here's where you put wheels under each goal so you can move it forward from intention to reality.

Because your goals are specific, you've got a visual picture of the desired outcome for each goal. You know how to measure whether the goal has been successfully accomplished. You know where the finish line is.

Now it's time to think through how to get there. For each goal, write down the actions you may need to take to accomplish that goal. Don't worry about getting actions in order at this point—just write them down. It's not uncommon to find that a fairly simple goal ("paint the sanctuary") actually requires dozens of steps, so allow plenty of time—and paper!

Once you've exhausted your list-writing, then circle those that seem necessary and non-negotiable. The circled items will be your Key Action Steps. If there's a step that, with reflection, seems unimportant, lightly cross it off. This is the "analyze and prune" process.

Next, get organized. Place your circled Key Action Items in a logical sequence. What step has to happen first? second? Keep rearranging steps until you think you've got them in order. As you examine the list of Key Actions, are there any that could be simplified? that should be broken into several steps? that can be dropped altogether?

Get organized by estimating the amount of time each step will take and deciding who will be primarily responsible for each step. Accountability requires you to have each goal measurable in terms of time, budget, and people's performance, so keep those elements in place as you create an action plan.

It's wise to take your action plan even further by determining what resources you'll need to accomplish each step. By thinking it through on paper you may find that "painting the sanctuary" requires you to have scaffolding up for two solid weeks—which presents significant problems for Sunday worship services. That piece of information will help you schedule the project for the least-disruptive time. And it lets you know that you'd better have the pastoral staff's input, too!

Throughout this Volunteer Leadership Series you'll be encouraged to move from the theoretical to the practical—to applying what you discover here to your unique church situation. Only you (and your team, if you have one) can create action plans for your church, because only you know all the factors that impact your possible actions. A course of action that makes great sense at one church might create more problems than it solves at another church.

Step 5: Create Job Descriptions

This is how you define the work to be done. It's also where you decide if the work will be done by paid staff or volunteers.

Written job descriptions are essential for sound volunteer leadership. It's no different than at a paid position: Without a job description there's no way to know what each person should be doing.

If you want to see what life without job descriptions is like, attend a pick-up volleyball game being played at a church picnic. Everyone knows what's supposed to happen—his or her team is supposed to knock the ball over the net in three hits or fewer. The ball is supposed to stay inside the boundaries drawn on the grass. You hit the ball back and forth until someone scores a point, and then you start over by serving the ball back into play. Simple.

So why is actually playing the game so difficult?

The answer is usually that while everyone has a *general* idea what to do, nobody is exactly sure what his or her *specific* job is. Balls land between players who thought it was someone else's job to hit the ball back. Someone in the back row mows over two players in an attempt to spike the ball from the front row. And players rotate positions, but nobody's quite sure when that's supposed to happen.

Chaos reigns on the court . . . and chaos can reign in your church, too.

When the assistant choir director takes it upon herself to change the order of service while the choir director is out of town, is that okay? Does she really have the authority?

If the volunteer janitor finds a leaking pipe one Friday afternoon, who does he call? Who's been deputized to call for a plumber?

And when there are two office assistants, whose job is it to fold all the bulletin covers—the job *nobody* likes to do?

Job descriptions answer those questions, and more besides. They nail down what duties the volunteer job includes, who the volunteer reports to, and how long the job will last. Job descriptions provide all the information a potential volunteer needs to know to make an informed commitment.

And if you'll go to the trouble to place your volunteer job descriptions on your church web site, you'll let potential volunteers have access to information about opportunities with just a few keyboard clicks. New members can see what jobs are already available—which often prompts inquiries about those jobs or jobs that aren't there but could be.

You'll find everything you need to know about creating job descriptions in volume 3.

Step 6: Recruit Volunteers

This topic is explored in depth in volume 4 of this Volunteer Leadership Series, but here's a sneak preview definition of recruitment:

Recruitment is an invitation to come discuss a volunteer role. It doesn't mean the person responding will necessarily get the job.

For many churches, this is a revolutionary approach to filling volunteer roles. Not everyone who signs up for a job automatically gets it. Recruiting *includes* marketing, but marketing isn't the most important part of the process. It's how you communicate your message, but not everyone who responds necessarily qualifies to be a volunteer.

Don't worry—being more selective about who you place as volunteers and more particular about where you place people doesn't hurt your program. It *helps,* as you'll discover that volunteers are happier, stay longer in their roles, and happily give positive testimonies about their volunteer participation.

If recruitment has become a necessary evil, or the least favorite of your responsibilities at church, I hope you're ready for a fresh perspective on placing people in volunteer jobs. When done right, it's a *ministry* that can bring about enormous spiritual growth in the lives of volunteers.

Volunteering can be rewarding for many reasons, some of which are described in detail in volume 4. If recruitment has become a dreaded duty or an unwelcome, frustrating chore, prepare for a welcome change!

Step 7: Interview Potential Volunteers

You can't do a good job of placing people in volunteer jobs without knowing about them . . . and actually *knowing* them.

Perhaps you use surveys to collect information. That's fine, but it's incomplete. In volume 4 you'll discover the value of conducting face-to-face interviews with potential volunteers. And you'll learn how to develop and train a team of interviewers who'll do the job with excellence.

A quick word about this step in the process: It's where a tremendous amount of ministry can happen in the span of 25 or 30 minutes as potential volunteers are heard and encouraged. At church we're very good at transmitting information, and we're often excellent when it comes to providing inspiration. But there's less opportunity for people to be heard—honestly, deeply listened to—by another person.

By interviewing potential volunteers you'll provide that blessing. Plus, you'll be equipped to recommend the right volunteer roles to each potential volunteer.

Step 8: Place Volunteers

How will you ensure effective matches between volunteers and opportunities? The activities included in this step provide the critical link between the volunteer, his or her ministry supervisor, and the ministry area in which the volunteer will work.

Think of this as that last ten feet between the Space Station and one of the shuttles bringing astronauts to the Station. Everyone knows that the fittings on both vehicles will join together. There's no question that everyone is motivated for the "docking maneuvers" to go well. But no matter how far the astronauts have flown to get on board the Space Station, if they can't navigate that last ten feet and make contact, they're not getting aboard.

You'll learn what you need to do to make the connection to everyone's satisfaction: the volunteer, the volunteer's supervisor, and the people who are served by the volunteer.

Placement is more than just sending a potential volunteer down the hall to check in with the church secretary or singles pastor. You'll get a detailed list of the steps that make placement a win-win situation for everyone in volume 4.

Step 9: Train and Support Volunteers

Getting the right person in the right job is just part of what it takes to have a successful volunteer ministry. You're not successful until the volunteer has become successful, too, and that takes training and support.

How will your church orient volunteers so they have the information they need and they feel comfortable? How will you equip volunteers with the skills they need to be effective? How will you provide support if problems arise?

It's wise for you to be asking those questions, because it's certain your potential volunteers are asking them!

In volume 5 you'll discover how to provide orientation and training for information . . . skills . . . culture . . . and values. The vast majority of volunteers want to do an excellent job in their volunteer role; it's important we give them every chance to do so.

Step 10: Recognize Volunteers

How will you thank volunteers for what they do? How often? Will you affirm and thank volunteers individually, or by teams? Those are just some of the questions you'll ask—and answer—in volume 6 of this Volunteer Leadership Series.

And you'll consider more than how to create centerpieces for the annual Volunteer Appreciation Banquet. You'll think about how to provide appropriate "payoffs" for different types of volunteers as you identify what motivates them.

Step 11: Supervise Volunteers

In the same way you expect to supervise paid staff, you need to supervise volunteers. This is especially important because volunteers generally *want* to be supervised. They *want* to get better at what they're doing. They view their volunteer jobs as important and significant. They need to know you feel the same way.

You may find that supervision includes . . .

Coaching—as you work with volunteers to create and track their performance against goals, action plans, and time lines. If you want to be able to delegate to volunteers it's critical that you ensure volunteers are prepared to see the tasks and responsibilities through.

Serving as a liaison—as you help the volunteer understand the church's overall mission, goals, and policies. And, conversely, you help ministry leaders understand a volunteer's concerns.

Mentoring—as you help connect a volunteer with resources and experiences that will help the volunteer grow. Typically, it's the ministry leader to whom a volunteer reports that will fill this role, but there may be elements of mentoring in your relationships, too.

Your goal is to see that each volunteer is supervised appropriately. It's almost never appropriate for *you* to be doing direct supervision. That role will be filled by the ministry leader who directly supervises each volunteer—but you need to see that it happens.

Step 12: Evaluate Volunteers

Most people hate being evaluated. We associate it with tests we've failed or annual meetings with a boss who has a long list of our failures to review. And because we dislike *being* evaluated, we're hesitant to *do* evaluations.

Your goal is to see that each volunteer supervisor is able and willing to evaluate volunteers in his or her area—and is equipped to do helpful evaluations, *positive* evaluations.

Generally, your contribution to the cause is to ensure that there's a clear job description for each volunteer job and that performance standards are equally clear. And you must train into supervisors of volunteers the notion that performance reviews are an ongoing process, not a quarterly or annual matter. If an employee is willing to improve anytime throughout the year, why mention areas where improvement is needed just once every three months? Praise—and encouragement to grow—need to come far more often.

Make evaluations discussions rather than lectures and you'll find that volunteers actually *enjoy* them. And so will you.

There are two things you want to cover in a volunteer evaluation . . .

1. *What are the volunteer's "well-dones"?* These are the things that a volunteer is doing well and that you'd love to see continued.

2. *What are areas in which the volunteer could improve?* We all have them, and sometimes we don't see them until someone gently points them out. Begin with the assumption that the volunteer genuinely wishes to be excellent in his or her service, and help the volunteer plan how to achieve excellence.

You may discover, in the course of an evaluation, that the volunteer isn't actually doing what's in his or her job description. Maybe the person initially came on board to lay out the monthly newsletter, but now that's done on computer. So the volunteer has been running the folding and stuffing machine instead. If there's a need to adjust a job description, the evaluation is a great place to do it.

Also, ask what would help volunteers better fulfill their roles and what resources are needed. Invite volunteers' suggestions about what might help your church better fulfill its mission and goals. What ideas do volunteers have for improving how things get done?

Volunteers' suggestions are worth their weight in gold, because volunteers see and hear things that will never reach your eyes or ears. Plus, giving volunteers permission to make suggestions removes the "I'm just a volunteer" mentality that keeps some volunteers from fully engaging.

> **"Volunteers' suggestions are worth their weight in gold because volunteers see and hear things that will never reach your eyes or ears."**

When you've got a homemaker, a Christian educator, and a mechanical engineer all volunteering in the nursery, they're seeing that experience from three very distinct perspectives.

The homemaker will suggest ways to make the nursery a warmer, more nurturing environment.

The Christian educator will find ways to use music and interaction with the babies to do teaching.

And the mechanical engineer will figure out a way to isolate dirty diapers in an airtight container within ten seconds of the diapers being removed from the babies.

They're all helpful contributions! Be sure you ask for those ideas—and that you empower volunteers to implement good ideas they generate.

How are you doing with these 12 steps of volunteer leadership? A little self-assessment can be healthy, so pause and fill out the chart on page 89. Complete the form yourself, but first make photocopies of the chart. Give a copy to your pastor and other staff members (if there are any), and also to some of your volunteers. Then see how the answers provided by others compare to yours.

Also, chart how the answers of paid church staff compare to the answers of volunteers. Do your staff think volunteers have everything they need to be effective, but volunteers don't share that perception? If you find there's a discrepancy between how staff and volunteers perceive life, that's a great reason to go open up a dialogue with staff about why changes must be made in your current volunteer leadership process.

Volunteer Leadership Assessment Survey

	Not Done At All	Needs Improvement	Done	Done Well
Vision				
We have a clear idea where we're going, and that idea is shared by our entire church leadership.	❏	❏	❏	❏
Mission and Purpose				
We have a clearly articulated mission and purpose statement. We know what God wants us to be and do in this place, at this time.	❏	❏	❏	❏
Objectives and Goals				
We know specific things we wish to accomplish and why accomplishing those things will help us fulfill our mission and purpose.	❏	❏	❏	❏
Action Plan				
We know how we'll get things done, when, and who is responsible for results.	❏	❏	❏	❏
Job Descriptions				
We have written job descriptions for every volunteer role.	❏	❏	❏	❏
Recruitment				
We're inviting people to come discuss volunteer roles.	❏	❏	❏	❏
Interviews				
We have an established procedure (and trained interviewers) for conducting one-on-one interviews with potential volunteers.	❏	❏	❏	❏

	Not Done At All	Needs Improve-ment	Done	Done Well
Volunteer Placement				
We have an established procedure for matching volunteers with specific volunteer opportunities.	❏	❏	❏	❏
Training and Support				
We have a volunteer orientation program in place and training programs that provide significant, needed information to volunteers.	❏	❏	❏	❏
Volunteer Recognition				
We have a planned, intentional calendar of group recognition events and/or a system for recognizing volunteers individually.	❏	❏	❏	❏
Supervision				
We have a system in place that provides each volunteer with competent supervision that helps volunteers develop and grow in their roles.	❏	❏	❏	❏
Evaluation				
Each volunteer is evaluated on a regular basis.	❏	❏	❏	❏

SIX
How to Carry the Vision Forward

Two approaches for moving the Vision for Volunteerism forward—one for pastors, one for other church leaders.

What you do next to turn the future you'd like to see— where volunteerism is a natural and common part of your church's experience—depends on who you are. That is, the next step for a pastor is different from the next step for a Sunday school superintendent or youth leader.

Here are some suggestions for both groups . . .

If you're a pastor looking for a church-wide volunteer leadership system that will bring about transformational change:

• Pray about it.

Your very next step is to pray daily about the direction you believe God is calling you. Urge other church leaders to pray, too. *Is* instituting a church-wide volunteer leadership system God's direction for your church right now?

• Do your homework.

Have leaders and some of your existing volunteers (both active and inactive) fill out the Volunteer Leadership Assessment Survey (page 89) and Attitude and Behavior Survey (page 72). Summarize the data so you're ready to report what you discovered.

• Schedule a meeting with stakeholders.

Invite volunteers, church leaders, everyone who might be impacted by changes in the volunteer leadership system. The purpose of these meetings is not to condemn or create guilt, but to gain insight into where you are now and where you want to be as a congregation.

Begin your meeting(s) with devotions. Consider letting your devotions flow out of Scripture, perhaps these passages: Deuteronomy 1:9-15; 1 Corinthians 12:14-27; Ephesians 4:11-16; 1 Peter 4:9-11; or 1 Peter 5:1-3.

• Prayerfully do some dreaming about your *what-ifs.*

Ask God to give you a clear and exciting vision for where you can be, and the impact you can have in your community. Prayerfully ask God to give you a vision that lines up with his will for your church, your membership, and his plans for your neighborhood and town. Humbly seek to accomplish God's purposes.

If the vision that emerges is to have a volunteer-friendly culture throughout your church, then make it a priority to begin *now* . . . knowing it may take three to five years to accomplish such a church-wide change.

• Select a task force to take responsibility for imple-mentation.

This topic will be covered in depth in volume 2, with step-by-step help to guide you through the process. You'll find photocopiable forms, as well as agendas for meetings. It's all there for you except for one thing—your willingness to turn over control of the process to someone else.

It may well be that you're not the right person to coordi-nate this effort. That's not a reflection on you personally; it's a recognition that as the pastor of your church you have other roles to fulfill. Plus, if the change is to be authentic through-out the church, having decisions made and implemented by lay people is essential.

The final outcome in a few years may not be precisely what you envisioned, or accomplished in quite the way you'd have done it, but it will be in place and powerful. Your church will have ownership of the process. And it will be successful and working.

Are you willing to trust your congregation to move ahead with something that's so important? After all, they're just volunteers.

By the way, if you're nodding in agreement with that last paragraph, please review the three theologies at the beginning of this volume. Your church members certainly *can* be trusted to do significant ministry! God wired them for it!

• Provide support and encouragement.

Your task force is going to hit some rough water along the way. It will be a wonderful contribution if you continually provide support for the project from the pulpit and in prayer.

If you're the leader of a ministry area and you're looking to transform just your corner of the church:

You'd like to change the entire congregation's view of volunteers and volunteerism, but that's beyond the scope of your abilities. Fine-tune the process in only your own ministry area and you'll see results in the lives of your volunteers and the lives they touch.

Here's how to move ahead implementing the volunteer leadership process in just the youth ministry area, or Christian education area, or wherever else you serve and lead.

• Begin with prayer.

Shifting how volunteers are brought on board and retained just *seems* like a small thing—it's huge! The impact will be felt church-wide even if you have nothing to do with another ministry area.

Volunteers will be treated differently in your piece of the organization. You'll do things for and with your volunteers that won't be part of every church volunteer's experience. You can expect to hear some questions about what you're doing and why. And you may discover that volunteers from other areas begin to migrate your direction.

And that will very quickly be noticed by other volunteer leaders.

How to Keep Anonymous Surveys Anonymous

You'll get more honest answers if survey responders trust that their responses will *truly* be kept anonymous—that you won't know who said what.

You can accomplish that by enlisting the help of a trusted person who is not closely associated with you. The pastor's secretary, for instance, or a trusted church layperson.

Along with the surveys include a note directing respondents to return their surveys to that trusted person, who will compile the information, re-key all written comments in a separate document, and then destroy all original surveys—without showing them to you.

Prayerfully ask God for both guidance and grace. Be sure your motivation is for the good of the volunteers you serve, not to "show the pastor how it's done" or to rustle a few volunteers away from other ministry areas.

Pray daily for guidance regarding which functions in the 12-step Volunteer Leadership System will offer the most help to your program. (It's often Volunteer Ministry Job Descriptions and Interviewing.) Confirm this with your present volunteers. Be realistic.

• Honestly fill out all the assessment tools in this chapter.

The Volunteer Leadership Assessment Survey (page 89) and Attitude and Behavior Survey (page 72) will give you huge insights—but not necessarily ones you enjoy. Ask some of your volunteers to anonymously fill out the surveys and compare their answers with your own. You may discover you don't understand life as volunteers in your church experience it.

• Prepare spiritually.

Do personal or team devotions that flow out of some of the passages listed on page 92. Let God speak to you about how he wants to use his church to impact the world. (Deuteronomy 1:9-15; 1 Corinthians 12:14-27; Ephesians 4:11-16; 1 Peter 4:9-11; or 1 Peter 5:1-3.)

• Watch for God's timing.

When you feel God's nudging, pursue one or two volunteer functions you want to add, or in which you want to improve volunteer participation. The resources you'll find in this series of books will help you.

• Keep moving ahead—but not alone.

Remember, one of our goals is that you not burn out. Getting volunteers to help you in significant ways is key to that goal. Volume 2 of this series will walk you through how to accomplish that task, and then to move on into gradually making the changes that will implement your vision for volunteerism.

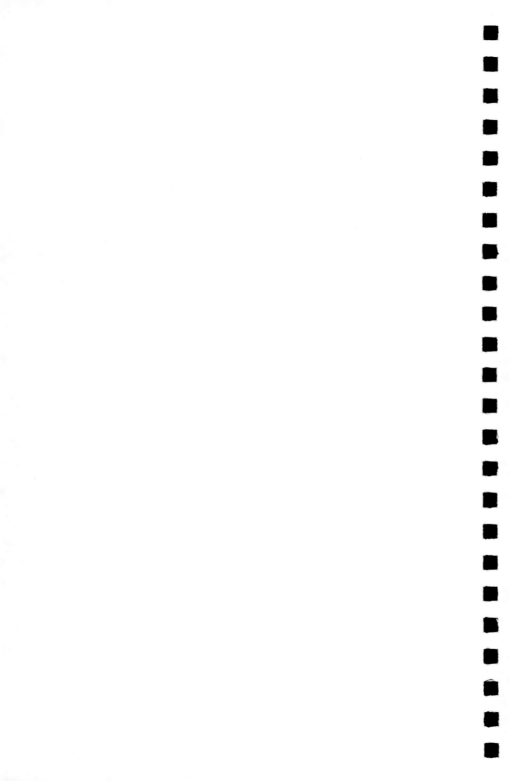

SEVEN
Let the Countdown Begin

Before you get to the "how-to's" of the rest of this series, here's one last chance to make sure you're ready for blastoff.

Maybe I'm showing my age, but I remember the days when space launches weren't everyday occurrences.

Astronauts were national heroes in America, and when a lift-off was scheduled, every television channel (all three or four of them!) canceled all other programming to have cameras trained on the rocket standing on the launch pad.

Commentators breathlessly followed the ticking of the countdown clock, and it wasn't until the booster rockets started to rumble and a voice counted down 10 . . . 9 . . . 8 . . . 7 . . . all the way to 1 that we knew for sure the switch had been pulled and the launch was a "go."

Well, your volunteer program is on the launch pad. Maybe you've already got an organized program, so it's presumptuous for me to assume that you're starting from scratch. For you, this is more like that time in a space launch when the massive booster rockets break off and fall back to earth. You're firing up your secondary rockets that will push you up and out of the gravitational pull that's holding you back.

Either way—whether you're taking off from the ground or making mid-course corrections—there's a universe out there to explore.

- You've got your vision set; you know where you want to go. You've suited up and have everything you need to push into the launch.

- You've considered the three theologies that are the foundation of a biblical approach to volunteer leadership.

- You've decided it's worth dealing with the personal change that's going to be required.

- You have determined if your church is volunteer-friendly and have thought through how to deal with any issues that have arisen.

- You've defined your preferred future as you've worked through the 12-step process. You're ready to carry the volunteer program forward.

So what could possibly be left to do before you move into the final countdown and push the switch to "launch"?

Just this: a final check, just like they run in the space program. There on the launch pad, with the astronauts strapped in and ready to go, just before the final launch sequence, there's yet one final check to confirm that everything is in place and prepared.

If you're absolutely sure you're set, skip ahead to the next volume in this series. But if you'd like one last confirmation that you're ready for launch, read through the following pages.

Ten
You've switched your paradigm about volunteer leadership.

If you have any reservations about the three theologies I discussed in chapter 1, settle them now. It's time to stop looking at volunteers as the means to an end: completing tasks.

Instead, volunteers *are* the end. Getting them involved in ministry is worthwhile in itself. Even if they don't complete tasks the way you'd like, on the schedule you'd prefer, they're growing in discipleship because of their effort and commitment.

Switching paradigms is often a matter of looking at a situation ("I've got to get stuff done and I have to use volunteers") with new values in mind.

For example, one summer I took a few weeks off from a hectic travel schedule. My intent was to get off airplanes and out of hotels for a while and enjoy my lovely mountain home west of Boulder. I determined that one thing I wanted to do to enhance my vacation at home was plant my rock garden with all kinds of lovely flowers.

The difficulty was that each year I'd planted flowers, deer came and ate them.

I went to the best mountain nursery in town and asked for the most deer resistant plants they had. One of the nursery workers designed a garden for me, then helped me plant the most spectacular garden I'd ever had. I also followed their expert advice on how to keep the deer away. This included adding blood meal to the soil, spraying the plants with Repel, and sprinkling everything with cayenne pepper.

For several days I sat on my deck, read, and looked down on my beautiful garden. Then I began to notice there were fewer and fewer flowers. I was mystified. I hadn't seen any herd of deer in my yard, but the flowers were steadily disappearing.

Then, one morning as I sat on the deck, I heard a funny wheezing, coughing sound. I looked down at my garden, and there was a deer chomping away at my flowers. Apparently she had asthma and couldn't smell a thing!

I began to wage a battle to save my flowers. I rushed out to the deck earlier and earlier each morning. I hated to leave my house for fear the asthmatic deer would again invade my flower garden and turn it into a salad buffet.

And all the time I was defending the garden I was missing the point that my vacation was being ruined. There wasn't any relaxing going on—not for me or the deer.

I finally realized I needed to change my paradigm. So, I went from thinking "flowers are beautiful" to "deer are beautiful." Then I relaxed, read, and watched my doe eat contentedly through my summer break.

That's when I became convinced of the power of paradigms!

Any paradigm shifting you feel convicted to do before we jump into the practical, how-to suggestions you'll find in volume 2? Now is the time.

The countdown has begun.

Nine . . .

You're ready to treat volunteers as full partners in ministry.

And not just you—everyone in leadership who will impact your volunteer program. You recognize that you're not "recruiting helpers" or "filling positions"; you're inviting members of the body of Christ to participate fully in service.

That may mean you need to teach some church leaders to delegate. You may have to renegotiate expectations on how tasks are accomplished. And you'll *definitely* need to see to it that volunteers receive the same respect that paid staff receive.

Part of what will fuel this change is a willingness of paid staff to incorporate in their definition of "success" the answer to this question: "How many people did we involve in the process?" We need to understand that encouraging a significant contribution from several people is often better than accomplishing the same task through the zealous efforts of one person. It's not more efficient. It's not necessarily cheaper. But it accomplishes more.

And consider how you define the words "ministry" and "service." Does it *have* to happen within your church building, or within your church's family of believers? What about a church member who serves through a community agency, or simply spends two evenings per week with a shut-in neighbor? Is that Christian ministry, too?

The answer varies from denomination to denomination and congregation to congregation. I've personally been made to feel like a deserter at times, especially when a ministry in

Let the Countdown Begin **101**

the community has been my primary focus. Some people didn't view that as "real church work." They still don't.

But today's church members seek validation for their ministry not only in church, but in the community, and also through their vocations and occupations.

After all, that's what being "in the world but not of it" is all about.

Eight

You're ready to help people discover their abilities, skills, and passions for ministry.

My friend Nancy Gaston shared this account with me from her work with volunteers at church:

"I conducted an interview with a woman who wasn't sure what she wanted to do. She was a retired home economics teacher but didn't care to teach.

"In the course of the interview she mentioned the church library—what a good collection of books we had, but how it seemed disorganized. Further questions revealed she knew little about organizing libraries but had always been fascinated by the process.

"With some instruction from a librarian and some printed materials, she learned to catalog and process all the new books and to supervise volunteers who kept the library organized and attractive.

"She agreed to 'try it for a year' and is still at it five years later—and loving the job."

Note that the job at which the retired home economics teacher excelled wasn't teaching Sunday school. It wasn't cooking for the church dinners. The job didn't actually *exist* until the woman identified it herself. It was her passion that recommended her for the position.

You're ready to help people discover their abilities, skills, and passions for ministry when you're ready to let *volunteers* lead you toward placement rather than letting open *positions* dictate what you'll recommend.

Still on the launch pad? Good—let's continue the countdown . . .

Seven . . .
You're ready to deal with organizational change.

I firmly believe the best possible way to do volunteer recruitment is through a centrally organized function: by establishing a Volunteer Director who interviews across the entire church and refers volunteers to various ministries.

But that may not be where you are. You may have neither the resources, time, or influence to make that happen. You may be the person who's struggling to get enough greeters at the doors each Sunday. What happens in the youth department may be the furthest thing from your mind.

Listen—as you institute changes you're launching your church on a journey. You've determined where you are, and you have a vision for where you want to be, so you've got a destination mapped out. All that's left to decide is how you want to go about getting there.

I once was giving a speech to a national conference of Methodist educators. Their theme was "The Christian Journey," and as part of my preparation I looked for a good definition of the word "journey." I discovered there were three general understandings of the word:

"Moving, progressing, trek, and pilgrimage" summarize the first understanding of "journey." This is a purposeful journey where you're making progress.

"Wandering, roaming, rambling, and drifting" summarize the second understanding. This is a journey that's somehow strayed off course. These journeyers are making progress . . . but they may not know where they're headed.

"Creeping, crawling, pussyfooting, or groveling" summarize the third understanding. This timid journeyer is barely making any progress at all—and may not *want* to make much.

I realized with amazement that I know people—and churches—who represent all three kinds of journeys. But what a difference how they take a journey makes in the destination they reach, and the fun and excitement they have getting there!

If you're beginning a journey of change, determine now what sort of a journey you want it to be. Do you want to move boldly and purposefully? ramble along? or plod along?

Wherever you are in your ministry of connecting volunteers with appropriate service opportunities, taking the next step will cause some disruption. Have you prepared spiritually? Are you praying? Did you skip over the suggestions that you do devotions on selected passages (see pages 92 and 94)? If you haven't meditated on those passages, do so before you go further. Let God's Word guide and sustain you through the rapids of change you'll likely encounter.

Six . . .

You're ready to be changed—personally.

In the Old Testament, God's message to the patriarch Abraham was, "You are blessed to be a blessing." For me, this statement sums up the rightful relationship between receiving and giving, and between beliefs and action.

I believe that each of us has been given unique abilities, skills, and passions. The true joy of these gifts is only realized when we share them with others. Hoarding or ignoring them brings nothing to anyone, including ourselves.

Once in a while we experience truly life-changing events. What's strange about these events is that on the surface they often appear to be ordinary, even mundane occurrences. Nothing amazing, nothing spectacular, nothing that makes a journal entrance.

Yet, when those moments come we somehow know that our life will never again be the same.

One of those events happened to me while I was reading an article in a denominational magazine. At the time it seemed I was just reading another couple of magazine columns, but my response to that article catapulted me out of my safe, comfortable church pew and into a hurting world.

The article was entitled "So You Ask Me What Is Poverty?" In it a woman who had lived in poverty all her life graphically described how being poor felt, tasted, and smelled—and how hopeless she felt as she watched her children become trapped in the same web of despair.

It has been more than three decades, but I remember that long-lost article ended with these words: "I did not come from another time. I did not come from another place. I am here, now . . . and there are others like me all around you."

Something in that woman's story spoke to my deepest being and made the command to be "doers of the word and not hearers only" come alive for me. I fell to my knees and prayed the only prayer possible, "I'm available, Lord. Show me what you would have me do."

Since that day, more than 35 years ago, I've been on an incredible journey of discovery. The Lord has led me, sometimes gently and sometimes by the scruff of the neck, to people and places in this world that are hurting. This journey began as I served as one of the volunteer founders and then executive director of an agency designed to match volunteers with the needs and resources of my community. We handled hundred of calls for help and found agencies, churches, or individual volunteers who provided what was needed. We also served as the connector between volunteers and more than 90 health, youth, senior, and welfare agencies. What an education—to finally learn about need in the specific versus thinking of it in the abstract.

My life was changed when I told God that I was available. Your life will change, too.

My life was changed when I became willing to serve people who want to do ministry in and through the church. Your life will change too.

Are you ready for a life change?

Good . . . because we're just about ready to blast off.

Five . . .
You're serious about getting every volunteer trained.

Adequate training takes more than lectures. There's mentoring involved, and time for people to grow into their responsibilities. There's direction and encouragement.

And there's a decision made by your church's leadership that adequate training is a priority worthy of funding and focus.

One of my favorite stories about training involves a teenage boy who was preparing to teach Sunday school for the first time. He was assigned to the four- and five-year-olds, and he took his new volunteer job seriously.

It was Wednesday night and already he was sitting at the kitchen table studying the lesson, highlighting sections, and writing notes in the margins of his lesson guide.

His mother came into the room and saw him concentrating fiercely, so she asked him what he was planning to teach.

"Well," he answered, "the lesson plan says to show the kids that each person is an individual with different potential and abilities; that each person is valuable for their particular capabilities. . . and that there is value in differences as well as conformity."

His mother was deeply impressed until her son then added with a sigh, "And if that doesn't work, I guess we'll make clay bunnies."

That young man knew *what* to do . . . but no idea how to actually *do* it. He wasn't trained to accomplish the job that had been delegated to him.

You're ready to do training, right? No clay bunnies for *your* children!

The countdown is even closer now . . . prepare for blastoff.

Four . . .
You're determined to do systematic, careful interviewing and placement.

There are shortcuts in every system, but when it comes to volunteer recruitment and placement, shortcuts are also shortchanges.

Skip interviewing and you shortchange every volunteer of the opportunity to be known and affirmed. You remove any way to collect the very information you most need to guide volunteers to the most appropriate places of service. And, if the truth be known, you remove one part of your job that's a lot of fun.

I'm guessing you're a "people person," someone who enjoys working with people more than working with things or manipulating data. That certainly describes most of the volunteer managers I've known through the years, though they're also able to create budgets and track people. But if left to their own devices, they'd rather spend time getting to know people and helping people.

Interviewing is where that begins. It's a valuable tool and great fun.

And if you place volunteers too quickly, or without their full involvement, you shortchange the volunteers and the people they'll be serving.

Trust me: You can do a poor job thanking volunteers and giving them the recognition they deserve, and many of those kind-hearted people will stick with you anyway. They'll hang in there because they find the job they're doing so rewarding.

But if you get a volunteer in the wrong job, you're doomed. The volunteer is doomed. It will be an unrewarding experience, and the volunteer won't find a good enough reason to stick.

Build a good system. Follow it. Don't settle for shortcuts.

Settle back in your seat. You're about ready for liftoff.

Three

You've decided it's worth the effort to see it through.

When you picked up this series you may have thought it held the silver bullet that would fix everything in your church with one simple action.

Unfortunately, that's not the case. If it were, you'd have undoubtedly done it yourself. My colleagues and I have absolute confidence that you're the right person in your church to do volunteer leadership. You care enough to launch the rocket or fine-tune your orbit. You want what's best for your volunteers and your congregation.

But you now know it won't be a quick, easy fix. There are systems to put in place, biases to weed out, and good habits to form. And it's not just for you—you need to have your entire leadership buy into the changes that are coming.

Is it worth it? Yes—for at least three reasons:

It's worth it for your volunteers. You'll mobilize volunteers and give believers a chance to plug into appropriate ministries. They'll grow, blossoming as they do what God designed them to do.

It's worth it for your community. We live in a hurting and unchurched world. We must learn to be the scattered church, reaching out to the communities in which we live. That reaching out begins within our communities of faith, but it stretches out beyond, too. You'll help your church's ministry move beyond the walls of the church, and believe me—those people need you.

It's worth it for your church. Do you know what the major difference is between the Red Sea—a life-giving body of water that teems with fish—and the Dead Sea, which kills fish almost instantly?

They're both seas. They both have streams feeding into them.

It's that the Dead Sea has no way for water to flow *out* of it. The salt and other minerals that are washed into the Dead Sea accumulate there and build in intensity. The Red Sea is fed by streams and also empties into others—and that gives the Red Sea life.

If your congregation is focused only on what happens within your walls, you're the Dead Sea. If you're pouring out the sparkling, God-inspired life you have into others, you're the Red Sea.

Share the life you've been given.

Do you feel the booster rockets rumbling beneath you?

Two . . .

You're determined to create a volunteer-friendly culture in your church.

It won't be quick. It may not be pretty. But it *is* achievable.

My experience says that authentic change may well take three to five years. You'll see dramatic improvements in your recruitment efforts as soon as you start using the 12-step volunteer leadership process my colleagues and I will share with you in this series of books.

But until your church's very culture changes, you're sticking little plastic bandages on deep, deep cancers. The temporary fixes are good, but they won't last unless your church leadership believes the three theologies I've outlined. Unless your congregation comes to understand that using their God-given abilities, skills, and passions for service isn't optional. Unless you're willing to embrace changes that will allow leadership to delegate thoroughly, volunteers to respond faithfully, and people to serve joyfully.

Are you ready? You're looking to create a place where what happened at a church I know can happen frequently at your church.

A retired woman had been an accountant for many years, and after retirement she didn't slow down a bit. She became deeply involved in community and church volunteering.

She said, "Now that I'm retired, I can give all my time to service and church-related projects . . . I don't give of myself because I 'should.' I don't like the word 'should' because that makes me feel I have to do something, and takes the joy out of it for me. I'm just selfishly doing what makes me happy."

Wouldn't you like to have a culture where people looked forward to getting involved as volunteers—because it made them happy?

The thunder you hear is the power of the rockets building thrust beneath you. You're nearly on your way to a grand adventure . . .

ONE . . .
You have a clear vision—and God's permission to get started.

Have you determined that God wants you to improve how volunteer leadership is done in your congregation? Do you know where you're headed?

If so, Godspeed. We're here to help.

Let nothing stop you.

God bless you.

Liftoff.

Core Values of Volunteer Leadership

- Every volunteer experience in the church should encourage a healthy relationship with Jesus Christ.

- We believe everyone in the body of Christ has something to give to the corporate body.

- Volunteers are respected as full partners in ministry.

- Volunteers can be any age.

- It's better to leave a volunteer position unfilled than to put the wrong person in the position.

- We provide the resources and training that volunteers need to be successful.

- It's okay for potential volunteers to say "no" to a request.

- Volunteer motivation and retention are outcomes of doing other things right.

- Volunteer leadership happens best when there's a centralized volunteer leadership function.

- Episodic volunteering is legitimate.

- We won't let volunteers burn out.

- The good of a local congregation supercedes the good of an individual volunteer.

- And we admit it: We can't motivate volunteers.